# Poland

Front cover: Malbork Castle

Right: Copernicus monument, Toruń

# TOP 10 ATTRACTIONS

**Kraków** The former capital of Poland is still the country's artistic and cultural centre and its most popular tourist destination *(page 32)*

**Tatra Mountains** With their spectacular peaks they are a hiker's paradise *(page 63)*

**Wieliczka Salt Mines** With its extraordinary, ornately carved chambers, this UNESCO World Heritage Site is a must-see *(page 55)*

**Warsaw** A truly capital city, where history and culture come alive *(page 70)*

**Zamość** Modelled on Italian trading cities, the Old Town is a 16th-century Renaissance jewel *(page 65)*

**Gdańsk** The birthplace of the Solidarity Movement *(page 90)*

**Sopot** Poland's frenetic summer capital *(page 100)*

**Malbork Castle** Built by the Teutonic Knights and one of Europe's largest fortified sites *(page 102)*

**Kazimierz Dolny** A confection of Renaissance and Mannerist houses *(page 69)*

**Wilanów Palace** This Baroque gem houses an impressive collection of portraits *(page 86)*

# CONTENTS

93

12

35

101

61

141

# INTRODUCTION

E ven though the country is more than 1,000 years old, Poland's survival is something of a miracle. Its boundaries were continually redrawn over the course of eight centuries. Then suddenly the nation disappeared from the map. Between 1795 and 1918, Poland, wedged in the middle of Europe, ceased to exist for the world's cartographers. Partitioned for a third time at the end of the 18th century by Prussia, Austria and Russia, Poland was reduced to a promise and a prayer for Poles, and the object of tug-of-war for more powerful states.

But that was only one aspect of Poland's troubles; then the real tragedy occurred. Hitler and the Nazis invaded Poland, launching World War II, then extinguished many of its cities and eradicated 20 percent of its people, including nearly its entire Jewish population of three-and-a-half million – until then the largest Jewish community in Europe. Wars have befallen many countries in modern times, but few have been as thoroughly ravaged as Poland.

Yet Poland rebuilt itself from the rubble of war. From photographs, paintings, architectural drawings and the memories of its grief-stricken survivors, Poles reconstructed the Old Towns of Warsaw and Gdańsk brick by brick, only to suffer four decades of Soviet-imposed Communist rule and grudging submission behind the Iron Curtain. Poland again rebounded.

In the 1980s, the trade union movement Solidarity *(Solidarność)* helped to trigger the demise of Communism in Poland and throughout the Soviet bloc. Poland has survived with its culture, language, spirit and most of its territory intact, and in 2004 it joined the European Union, as a modern, independent nation.

The Podhale region and the Tatra mountains

## Historic Cities

Largely rural, Poland has great tracts of wilderness and primeval forest in its 22 national parks. However, the country is perhaps best known for ancient towns rich in history and architecture. Kraków, which survived unscathed from the war, is a splendid medieval city (it was the royal capital for 500 years), with a magnificent market square, castle complex on a hill, and one of Europe's oldest, most prestigious universities.

Warsaw, Poland's largest city by far and its commercial and political capital, is not the bleak grey morass of Communist days. It may still be a little harsh on the eyes in places, but it is undeniably beautiful in others, and perhaps best expresses Poland's current crossroads. A 20-minute walk can take you from the Royal Castle to a monolith of Stalinist architecture to the gleaming headquarters of international companies banking on Poland's emergence as a major European player.

While Warsaw's Old Town is an astonishing phoenix-like fable of reconstruction, Gdańsk's historic centre is even more alluring, its Royal Way a loving restoration that defies the imagination. No matter how many times you stroll through the medieval layouts of these cities over cobblestoned streets, gazing at stunning examples of Gothic, Renaissance and Baroque architecture created, incredibly, as late as 1953, you cannot help but be amazed. The buildings look genuinely old; it is as though the indefatigable Polish people willed their authenticity.

Smaller towns can be just as impressive. Zamość is a perfect Renaissance town with one of the most photogenic main squares in the country. Zakopane is an Alpine-style town carved out of wood at the foot of the High Tatras, the highest peaks of the Carpathian Mountains, within easy range of great hiking and skiing. Toruń, the home of the great astronomer Nicholas Copernicus, is a feast of red-brick Gothic architecture, while Poznań, a determined trade centre, combines commerce with authenticity in its extraordinary Old Market Square.

## Population and Religion

Poland is a nation of a little under 39 million, the size of Spain. Its people are fervently Catholic – over 80 percent call themselves practising Catholics – and more conservative than many of their Western European neighbours. Throughout most of its history, Poland was an intensely cosmopolitan place, with Germans, Jews, Lithuanians, Belarusians, Armenians and others living within its borders. During the Second Republic (1919–39), only two-thirds of the people were ethnic Poles. It has also traditionally been a land of religious tolerance. When medieval Europe was rocked by religious wars, Poland was a safe haven for Jewish, Protestant and Orthodox refugees – making the intolerance later inflicted by Germany on Polish territory all the more terrible.

Today, Poland is unusually homogenous in terms of ethnicity: some 98 percent of the people are Poles. The Jewish pop-

More than 80 percent of Poles are practising Catholics

ulation was reduced to 250,000 after World War II, and today there are only a few thousand Jews living in Poland. The largest minority groups are Lithuanians, Ukrainians and Belarusians.

Literacy rates are high, at a shade under 100 percent. Poles are well-educated, and young people in the larger cities speak English (much more so than German or Russian) with the same fluency and enthusiasm of those a couple of border lines west. They're up-to-date on fashions, trends and music; they have mobile phones glued to their ears and e-mail accounts they tap into daily at internet cafés across the country.

## Rural Poland

Of course, the vast Polish countryside is a very different story. Here you'll still see a stubbornly traditional way of life that seems years, if not decades, slower than city life. Little-trafficked roads are lined with wooden shrines, erected

**Wolin National Park**

by people intent on mani-
festing their devotion. Even
if you're not planning on
travelling through the countryside, you can get a good
taste of rural life by visiting
a *skansen*, or outdoor ethno-

**Green Poland**

Almost one third of
Poland is covered by forest,
mostly pine, spruce and
mixed deciduous and
coniferous trees.

graphic museum, which makes the ways of Polish country
life accessible by relocating historic houses and farm buildings from small villages to open-air exhibitions.

## A Blend of East and West

Poland's history as a territory coveted by great powers all
around it ensured that the north–south divisions often seen
elsewhere are, here, primarily east–west divisions. The west
is more Germanic, organised, pragmatic and industrious,
while the East has a reputation of being more Russian –
which means, in short, relaxed, cultural and introspective.
Poznań, for example, halfway between Berlin and Warsaw,
revels in its business skills and organisational attitude.
Kraków, the ancient capital much closer to Ukraine than Germany, is just as proud of its free-flowing cultural prowess
and its status as a place where art and education override
business (except, of course, for the business of tourism).

There has always been a cultural struggle between East and
West in Poland. The Poles are a Slavic people, like their
Ukrainian and Russian neighbours to the east. Yet their historical and cultural connections to the West are formidable.
The Catholic Poles first took their religious cues from the West
in the 10th century, and cultural epochs basic to Western Europe – the Enlightenment and the Renaissance, for example –
were just as much a part of Polish society. The shared identity, as well as the uneasy conflicts, between East and West have
defined this land in ways that go far beyond geography.

The spa town of Jelenia Góra

## A Nation of Triumphs

Although Poland has suffered a chequered political past, it has been the source of glorious achievements in the arts and sciences. Poland claims such greats as the composer Frédéric Chopin, the novelist Joseph Conrad, Marie Curie (Nobel Prize winner in chemistry and physics) and the Nobel Prize winners in literature Henryk Sienkiewicz, Władysław Reymont, Wisława Szymborska and Czesław Miłosz. In 1932 the country was the first to crack Germany's Enigma code, a feat many believe to have shortened World War II by at least three years and to have prevented a nuclear holocaust in Europe.

## Life Post-Communism

Though by most measures, Poland, along with Hungary and the former Czech Republic, has made incredible strides in the years since the break-up of Communist Europe in 1989, many of its citizens and international institutions feel that the transition to privatisation and democracy has not been as smooth or as rapid as might have been hoped. Immediately after gaining political and economic freedom in 1989, Poland found itself without state support, and production plummeted. While there was a huge spurt in growth and prosperity in the mid-1990s, unemployment has recently increased dramatically. However, with Poland now a member of the European Union (EU), the gap between Western and Central Europe is at last closing.

Yet Poles remember the past and the often-fractured road that has brought them to this point. They are intensely proud that Copernicus, who 'stopped the sun and moved the Earth' and revolutionised the way we understand our universe, was a Pole. They revel in the fact that Poland signed the second-oldest Constitution delineating government powers, after the United States. Poles young and old live with the horrors of death-camp atrocities committed on their soil. They turned out in great adoring hordes for the late Pope John Paul II, known to them as Karol Wojtyła, former Archbishop of Kraków. And the Polish people recognise the role that a little-known shipyard electrician in Gdańsk by the name of Lech Wałęsa had, first as a leader of the Solidarity union and then as Poland's first elected president since 1922, in indelibly changing the events of the second half of the 20th century. Poland may only now be developing as a destination for many of the world's travellers, but it is certainly no stranger to the world stage.

## Chopin

Frédéric Chopin (1810–49) was born in Żelazowa Wola, just outside Warsaw, to a French father and Polish mother. He spent his youth in the capital but also learned all the folk songs and dances of the surrounding villages, which he utilised in almost all his later works. He made his debut as a classical pianist when still a boy, playing in elegant salons. In the autumn of 1830, he left Warsaw, then a small, autonomous duchy (though ultimately under the control of the Russian Tsar) and when the Russians occupied the duchy the following year, Chopin settled in Paris. In 1836 he met the novelist George Sand, who looked after him during his years of ill health, and he travelled with her to Majorca. His health continued to deteriorate, however, so he returned to France. In 1847, George Sand left him. Lonely, ill and poor, he fled to London, where he gave his last public performance. Returning to Paris, he died of tuberculosis.

# A BRIEF HISTORY

Poland's war-torn, almost incomprehensibly fractured history plays out like an epic novel – occasionally triumphant, frequently sad and tragic. Over a millennium, Poland evolved from a huge, economically powerful kingdom to a partitioned nation that ceased to exist on world maps for over 120 years, and finally to a people and land at the centre of the 20th century's greatest wars and most horrific human tragedies. But Poland has survived, with its culture, language and most of its territory intact, and today Poles, newly entered into the European Union (EU), are taking their place at the forefront of post-Communist Central Europe.

## Foundations of the Polish State

The region that would become Poland, a great plain sandwiched between the Vistula and Odra rivers, has been inhabited since the Stone Age by migratory tribal peoples – among them Celts, Balts, Huns, Slavs and Mongols. Tribal culture reigned, untouched by the more sophisticated civilisation of the Roman Empire. Slavic tribes arrived by the 8th century AD and put down roots; the Ślężanie, Mazowszanie, Pomorzanie and Wiślanie peoples inhabited much of the territory. The Polonian tribe, which settled the area that today is western Poland around Poznań, provided the foundations for the development of a Polish language and nation.

Prince Mieszko, leader of the Piast dynasty that ruled the Polonians, undertook the bold step of unifying the

### What's in a name?

The Polanie tribe (the Polonians), who lived in the Warta valley not far from Poznań, were the people who gave Poland its name. Polanie means 'of the fields'.

Polanie (literally, 'people of the fields') and neighbouring tribes. Mieszko adopted Christianity – most likely a savvy political move to place the new state on equal footing with nearby Christian states with ties to Rome – and married a Czech princess, Dobrava, in 965. His religious conversion won him the support of the papacy, and Mieszko effectively founded the Polish state the following year. By the end of the 10th century, he had united his tribal territory, Wielkopolska (Great Poland), with that of another tribe, Małopolska (Little Poland) – regional names that remain in use today. Silesia, settled by a different tribe, would eventually become the third component of the nascent Polish state.

Stained-glass window, Franciscan Church, Kraków

Mieszko's son Bolesław 'The Brave' was crowned by Otto III, the Holy Roman Emperor. Bolesław later repelled invasions from Otto's successor and then sought Poland's own expansion eastwards; he eventually annexed parts of present-day Ukraine. The Pope recognised Bolesław as the first king of Poland in 1025, elevating the country to full membership in a European community of Christian states.

Duke Bolesław Krzywousty divided the country into four provinces to be ruled by his sons. Kraków grew in importance and eventually became the country's capital in the 12th century (replacing Gniezno in 1038), when Duke Bolesław 'the Wry Mouthed' established his official residence on Wawel Hill. Kraków was better positioned for trade and also less vulnerable to attacks from the Czechs and Germans. Helped by the arrival of immigrants from all over Europe, including thousands of Jews, Kraków became a prosperous and culturally enriched capital.

Beginning in the mid-13th century, Tartars invaded Poland on three occasions. Threatened by the Prussians, Duke Konrad of Mazovia invited in the Order of the Teutonic Knights to help defend against them. The Knights used their considerable military might to then assume control of the very territory they had helped defend, capturing Gdańsk, securing most of the Baltic region and cutting off the rest of Poland from access to the sea. The Tartars defeated the Poles at the Battle of Legnica and destroyed most of Kraków, leaving only the castle and St Andrew's Church intact.

## The Teutonic Knights

The Teutonic Knights were a military order of German knights who served in the Holy Land. They played an important part in Polish history, originally acquiring their prosperity through gifts of land for their hospital work during the Crusades. They were also given land in northeast Poland in 1225 in return for assisting the Mazovian Duke Konrad to repel an invasion of pagan Prussians. After annexing this Prussian territory, they gradually extended their occupation, invading Polish towns such as Gdańsk in the early 14th century and slaughtering the inhabitants, until their incursions were finally repulsed by the joint Polish-Lithuanian Commonwealth, and they were defeated in 1410 at the Battle of Grunwald. Malbork Castle (see page 102), established as the headquarters of the Knights' grand master, was taken over by the Poles in 1457 and the grand master swore allegiance to the Polish king.

## Kazimierz the Great and the Jagiellonians

The last king of the Piast dynasty, Kazimierz the Great, succeeded in reunifying Poland. His rule ushered in Poland's first golden age. Kazimierz built great castles and towns, codified laws, and created an entire administrative system of governance for the war-torn country. He rebuilt Kraków with magnificent architecture and established the country's first university there. Kazimierz, a pragmatist, did not try to wrest control of Silesia, in the hands of Bohemia, or the territory seized by the independent state of the Teutonic Knights. Instead, he consolidated the state by expanding eastwards and accepting minority populations, including persecuted Jews from across Europe, into the predominantly Catholic nation.

Malbork Castle

Kazimierz's death in 1370 left the crown to his nephew, Louis of Anjou, the King of Hungary. One of his daughters, Jadwiga, succeeded Louis in Poland, while the other assumed control of Hungary. Jadwiga's 1386 marriage to Jagiełło, the Grand Duke of Lithuania, led to Poland's strategic alliance with that powerful country. Following his wife's death, Jagiełło ruled both Poland and Lithuania for just shy of half a century, establishing a dynasty that would remain in power until 1572. The united countries defeated the Teutonic Knights at the Battle of Grunwald in 1410, halfway between Warsaw and the Lithuanian border, and repelled Germanic eastward expansion. The Thirteen Years' War yielded great benefits for Poland: the transformation of Danzig (Gdańsk) into an independent city-state under the protection of the Polish crown and the capture of other Knights' territories.

Polish nobles saw their political might expand in the early Renaissance with the king's 'rule of the nobility', which granted exclusive right to enact legislation to nobles in the parliament, or Sejm. The 1500s saw prosperity, power and cultural and scientific achievement for the Polish-Lithuanian Commonwealth. In 1543 Mikołaj Kopernik (Nicolaus Copernicus), born in Toruń and a graduate of the Jagiellonian University in Kraków, published his groundbreaking treatise, *De Revolutionibus Orbium Coeliestium*, which positioned the sun and not the earth as the centre of the uni-

Monument to the Battle of Grunwald

verse. Although the Reformation and Lutherism had an impact on Poland, the country largely avoided the devastating religious wars that raged elsewhere in Europe.

The Sejm moved to Warsaw in 1569, and the death of the last ruler of the Jagiellonian dynasty, Zygmunt August, led to the creation of a Republic of Nobles and an elective monarchy that would serve it. Warsaw, better located in the centre of the country, became the official capital in 1596. King Zygmunt Waza (Sigismund Vasa) moved there from Kraków in 1609.

## Swedish Dynasty

Three successive elected kings emerged from the Swedish Waza dynasty. Sweden had become the strongest military power in Europe after the Thirty Years' War and in the mid-17th century the country set its expansionist sights on Poland. The Swedes invaded Poland in 1648, an event labelled the Swedish Deluge in Polish history books. The devastating war lasted five years, during which time Sweden was able to capture most of Poland. The war and the disastrous effects of the plague decimated the population of Poland, reducing it to just 4 million, roughly half its total in the early 17th century.

Remarkably, Poland retained enough military might to repel the Ottoman Turks in their advance through the Balkans. The military leader Jan Sobieski defeated Turkish troops at the Battle of Chocim in 1673, and Sobieski would later be credited with saving Vienna from Turkish forces (and thwarting the Ottoman Empire's designs on Western Europe). Sobieski was elected king of Poland in 1674, but his attention to battles against the Turks at the expense of domestic affairs did not bode well for him and Poland.

## Decline and Partitioning

At the start of the 18th century, Poland entered a prolonged period of decline, marked by financial ruin, a debilitated army, and a series of ineffectual kings. Poland was transformed into a client state of the Russians, and then lost much of its western territory to the Prussians during the Silesian Wars that ended in 1763. The following year Stanisław August Poniatowski was elected the last king of the Polish-Lithuanian Commonwealth, and Poland soon faced one of its most humiliating episodes.

The powerful Prussians came up with a plan to partition Poland, which gained the support of the Russians. The imposed treaty in 1772 robbed Poland of nearly a third of its lands. Yet Poniatowski recovered to preside over a reform movement that precipitated the creation of the 1791 Con-stitution, which restored the hereditary monarchy and over-hauled Poland's political system. The liberal constitution, the oldest in the modern world after that of the United States, provided for the separation of powers among legislative, judicial and executive branches of the government.

None of these reforms pleased the Russians and Prussians, who continued to covet Polish territory. Russia invaded Poland and in 1792–3 it, along with Prussia, imposed a sec-ond partition of Poland, annulling the constitution and es-sentially divvying up the country between them. Tadeusz Kościuszko, a hero of the American War of Independence, led a military insurrection in 1794, defeating the Russians with a mostly peasant army. The uprising was quashed, however, and in 1795, Poniatowski was forced to abdicate. A third par-tition crushed Poland and placed the country under the con-trol of Austria, Prussia and Russia. Poland ceased to exist for the next 123 years. Warsaw went to Prussia, Kraków to the mighty Austrian empire.

In desperation, Poland looked to Napoleon Bonaparte and Revolutionary France for assistance against its oppressors. Napoleon defeated the Prussian army in several key battles and established a semi-independent Duchy of Warsaw from 1807 to 1815. Napoleon gained an ally in Józef Poniatowski,

The Cossack massacre during the January Uprising, 1863

a heralded military leader and the nephew of the last king. The 1812 Polish War re-established the Poland–Lithuania border, but Napoleon's troops were crushed as they advanced on Moscow. Napoleon suffered a great defeat, but his ally Poniatowski refused to surrender, preferring to sacrifice himself and his troops. The suicidal mission became an important rallying cry for Poles during the remainder of the 19th century.

The Congress of Vienna of 1815, which aimed to reorganise Europe after the Napoleonic Wars, did not re-establish an independent Poland. Rather, it re-partitioned the country, placing the Duchy of Warsaw under the control of the Russian tsar. For three decades, Kraków existed as an independent city-state, though it was incorporated into the Austrian partition in 1846.

The former Duchy of Warsaw, called the Congress Kingdom, enjoyed some autonomy and prosperity in the early 19th century. Poles launched a series of armed insurrections against its occupiers in 1830 and, after defeat, again in

1846 and 1863. The last rebellion counted on support from England and France that never arrived. Many Poles, fearful that an independent Poland would never again be realised, emigrated to France and then the United States during this period. Those who remained focused on preserving Polish language and culture, if not the Polish state.

### Pianist and PM

In 1918 the acclaimed concert pianist, Ignacy Jan Paderewski (1860–1941), became Poland's first prime minister. He later lived in exile in the United States.

## The Aftermath of World War I

The next pivotal episode in Polish history coincided with the end of World War I and the defeat of the Russians, Germans and Austrians. The partition of Poland collapsed in 1918, and Poland's bid for independence won the support of both American president Woodrow Wilson and the Bolshevik government in Russia. The Polish war hero Józef Piłsudski (1867–1935), released from a German prison, took control of Poland. In 1920, the Soviets invaded, but Piłsudski and his troops managed to stop the advance at the Vistula and went on to occupy parts of Ukraine and Lithuania.

In 1926, Piłsudski engineered a military coup and seized control under the Sanacja, or senate, government that would rule until the start of World War II. By 1933, Poland was sandwiched between two dictatorships: Stalin in Russia on the eastern border, and Hitler in Nazi Germany to the west. Both fixed their eyes on occupying Poland, and they signed the ruthless Nazi–Soviet Pact on 28 August 1939, which stated that either would be free to pursue expansionist acts without the interference of the other. In the agreement was a secret clause providing for the eventual full partition of Poland between Germany and Russia – even though Poland had signed 10-year non-aggression pacts with both.

## Nazi Invasion, World War II and the Holocaust

On 1 September 1939, the Nazis invaded Poland. The annexation of Danzig (modern day Gdańsk) marked the official start of World War II. Soon after, German forces launched an occupation of Kraków, where they based their governing body, and laid siege to Warsaw. The Soviets invaded Poland less than two weeks later on 17 September, following the terms of the pact signed with Germany.

The Nazis initiated a ruthless campaign in 1940, rounding up intellectuals, Jews and others, executing some in the streets and deporting others to concentration camps in the occupied territory. Craftsmen and labourers were deported to do forced labour in the Reich. Artists, scientists and priests were taken into 'protective custody', which was often a synonym for concentration camps. The Germans constructed walled Jewish ghettoes in Warsaw and Kraków. At death camps such as

Hitler's bunker, known as 'the Lair', at Kętrzyn

Auschwitz *(see page 57)*, near Kraków, the Nazis eventually murdered millions of Poles, as well as other prisoners from across Europe. The Soviets themselves imprisoned some 1.5 million Poles in labour camps of their own and eliminated potential 'troublemakers' through actions like the Katyn massacre in 1940, in which an estimated 15,000–20,000 Polish military officers and civilians were summarily executed.

From 1941–5 Poland was under Nazi occupation, and the country became the focus of Hitler's campaign to exterminate Jews and non-Aryans. Hitler invaded the Soviet Union in 1941, an act that drew the Soviets and Poles together in a shaky alliance.

Monument to the Warsaw Uprising, Warsaw

A heroic uprising in 1943, led by poorly armed Jews in the Warsaw ghetto, lasted a month until Nazi reinforcements annihilated it and reported back to Germany that 'Warsaw's Jewish quarter has ceased to exist'. The following year, Poland's Home Army initiated a surprise attack against the occupying Nazis in Warsaw, and awaited assistance from the Soviet Red Army, perched on the outskirts of the capital. The military support never came, and as his troops left the city after quashing the insurgency, Hitler ordered them to raze Warsaw building-by-building and thereby annihilate important monuments of Polish culture. When the Soviets entered the city, they found it reduced to rubble and ashes.

World War II was more devastating for Poland than any other country. Six million Poles lost their lives during World War II, and the Jewish population was decimated, reduced from three million to just a couple of thousand. Poland lost a significant amount of territory after new borders were drawn up in the Yalta Agreement of February 1945, including the eastern regions around Wilno (Vilnius) and Lwów (Lvov). The Polish borders shifted west a couple of hundred kilometres, incorporating ancient parts of Silesia like Wrocław, the German city of Breslau before the war. Poland also regained Danzig, not a part of Poland since its seizure by the Teutonic Knights. The city reverted to its original Polish name, Gdańsk.

## Communism and Soviet Domination

In the aftermath of the war, Poland was Sovietised, with the installation of a Soviet-friendly communist regime, the nationalisation of businesses, confiscation of church property, and

### Catholic Resistance

The fiercely religious Roman Catholic Church was one of the few institutions that retained a level of independence in Communist Poland, a fact that led to Stalin famously comparing imposing Communism on the Poles to putting a saddle on a cow. The Communists did their best however, regarding the Church as a reactionary relic of the pre-war system. Repression was severe: priests and laymen alike were openly attacked and constantly threatened with arrest by the government, and by 1950 the financial assets of the Church had been confiscated. In 1952, one of the heroes of this frightening era, Cardinal Stefan Wyszyński, the primate of Poland, was arrested for his anti-state attitudes. He was exiled to a monastery where he was held prisoner for three years.

Palace of Culture, Warsaw

forced exile of political and religious leaders. With Soviet aid, a rebuilding programme was initiated, an effort that reconstructed the Old Towns of Warsaw and Gdańsk, among others, in costly and meticulous efforts based on paintings, photographs and architectural drawings. The Soviet Union signaled its domination over Poland with the 1955 'gift' of the Palace of Culture and Science in Warsaw, a vast skyscraper that would become a hated symbol of foreign influence.

Many Poles, especially among the intellectual and professional classes, opposed Soviet influence and Communist rule, and in 1956 the regime faced its first real test. Worker strikes and protests erupted in Poznań, and spread into armed confrontations in the streets. Security forces opened fire on rioters and killed some 80 people. A weakened and suddenly unstable Communist Party installed former First Secretary Gomułka as leader without consulting Moscow, an event that prompted Soviet, East German and Czech troops to amass on the Polish borders. A similar uprising occurred in Hungary the same year, and the Soviets invaded to quickly crush it.

But the episode in Poland, called Polish October, exposed cracks in the Communist regime, and served as the impetus for a slight relaxation of censorship, religious repression and economic controls. Reforms stalled, however, and the following decade saw a return to strict Soviet doctrine. The 1970s were marked by inflation and the emphatic snuffing of strikes and protests. Living standards dropped dramatically, and the Soviet Union was forced to prop up the Polish economy.

## Pope John Paul II and Solidarity

In August 1978, the Polish Cardinal and Archbishop of Kraków Karol Wojtyła was elected Pope; he took the name John Paul II. A staunch opponent of the Communist regime, Wojtyła returned to Poland from Rome in 1979 as Pope and drew great, thunderous crowds at every stop. The following year, unrest grew among workers after massive increases in food prices. Lech Wałęsa, a shipyard electrician, led strikes in Gdańsk. The size and vehemence of their protests, which spread countrywide, forced the government to negotiate with the Solidarność (Solidarity) trade union, granting its workers' demands and allowing free trade unions limited autonomy to oversee their industries. With hindsight, Solidarity was critical in establishing the foundations for opposition to Communist rule across Central and Eastern Europe.

General Wojciech Jaruzelski adopted a hard line and declared martial law in December 1981 in response to continued strikes across Poland. He initiated a military takeover of the Communist Party, and the government arrested thousands of Solidarity activists and sympathisers, banned the trade union and suspended civil rights. Two years later, the regime lifted martial law after the Pope John Paul's second visit to Poland, and Lech Wałęsa won the Nobel Peace Prize in 1983, familiarising the world with the struggles of Polish workers.

The government's resolve did not waver, however. In 1984, the Polish secret police murdered Father Jerzy Popiełuszko, an outspoken supporter of Solidarność.

The mid-1980s witnessed a gradual programme of liberalisation in Poland on the heels of Mikhail Gorbachev's

*perestroika* and *glasnost* in the Soviet Union, the promises of greater openness and economic freedoms. The economic crisis in Poland persisted, though, and mass strikes were staged, even as Gorbachev visited Poland. In 1989, talks established the basis for limited power-sharing between the Communist Party and Solidarity.

Polish Parliament in session

## The End of Communist Rule

Desperate austerity measures failed to jump-start the economy. In semi-free elections, Solidarity was the overwhelming victor, and the Communist regime collapsed. On 9 December 1990, Poles made Lech Wałęsa the first popularly elected president in post-World War II Poland. In 1991, Wałęsa met the Pope in the Vatican. That same year, the Warsaw Pact was dissolved.

Poland's road to capitalism and democracy has been a complicated one. Wałęsa fell out of favour with Poles and was defeated in the 1995 elections. But by that time, the country had joined the World Trade Organization, and the EU had agreed to open negotiations to admit Poland.

Poland joined NATO in 1999 and the EU five years later. Huge crowds turned out for John Paul II's eighth visit to his homeland in 1999, and his death in 2005 was widely mourned; both signs that Poland's committed Catholics and fervent patriots had survived Communism with their faith and pride intact. In 2005 Lech Kaczynski of the Law and Justice party became president and a year later his twin brother Jarosław became prime minister. This double act ended in 2007 with the latter's defeat by the pro-Western Donald Tusk.

# Historical Landmarks

**966** The founding of Poland.

**992** Bolesław I Chrobry (the Brave) is crowned first king of Poland.

**1309** The Teutonic Order rules over a large territory along the Eastern Baltic Sea, including Gdańsk.

**1325** Polish-Lithuanian alliance is formed against the Teutonic Knights.

**1333** Kazimierz III Wielki (Casimir the Great) doubles the size of his realm, expanding to the east and transforming Poland into a multinational state.

**1364** Founding of Kraków University.

**1386** Founding of the Jagiellonian dynasty.

**1410** Teutonic Knights are defeated at the Battle of Grunwald; Poland becomes a more powerful, unified realm.

**1543** Nicolaus Copernicus publishes *De Revolutionibus Orbium Coelestium*.

**1569** Poland and Lithuania are united into a single Commonwealth.

**1655–60** Sweden invades Poland.

**1673** Jan Sobieski defeats the Turks at the Battle of Chocim.

**1772, 93, 95** Partitions divide Poland among Prussia, Austria and Russia.

**1918** Independent Polish state created after the end of World War I.

**1939** German troops invade Poland, triggering World War II.

**1943** Warsaw Ghetto Uprising.

**1944** Warsaw Uprising by Polish Home Army; city is razed by the Nazis.

**1945** After the end of World War II, new borders are established by the victorious Allies. The Communists take power.

**1956** Troops crush anti-government riots in Poznań.

**1981** Martial law is proclaimed after disturbances spearheaded by the trade union Solidarity (Solidarność), led by Lech Wałęsa.

**1990** Lech Wałęsa wins presidential election.

**1993** The former Communists defeat Solidarity in parliamentary elections.

**1999** Poland becomes a member of NATO.

**2004** Poland joins the European Union (EU).

**2005** Polish-born Pope John Paul II dies.

**2006** The conservative Law and Justice party forms a majority coalition.

**2007** Donald Tusk takes office as prime minister on 16 November.

# WHERE TO GO

Poland, bordering the Baltic Sea to the north, Germany to the west, the Czech Republic and Slovakia to the south, and Ukraine, Belarus, Lithuania and Russia to the east, is large and predominantly rural. The main points of interest for first-time visitors are the principal cities, beginning with Kraków, Warsaw and Gdańsk – whose old towns certainly rank among the finest of Central Europe, or Europe, for that matter – and smaller, well-preserved towns that are rich in history, architecture and Polish character. It is also a place to see great castles, memorials of Jewish culture that mark unspeakable tragedy, and churches and synagogues that are sites of important Catholic and Jewish pilgrimage.

It's easy and inexpensive to get around Poland by train, probably the preferred method of navigating the country. Exploring the Polish countryside, which seems several decades, if not more, behind the cities, requires either a lot of time and patience, or a car. And even one's personal transport can be slow-going, as the Polish road system lags behind its speedy development in other areas. For visitors with plenty of time, the mountains, sea and lake districts have much to offer, but this guide deals primarily with the major Polish cities and towns.

Because Kraków is the country's most popular tourist destination, this section begins there, in southeast Poland. Just beyond Kraków, reached in easy day trips, are the fantastic 700-year-old Wieliczka salt mines and the horrendous physical legacy of the Nazi concentration camps of Auschwitz. In southern Poland, along the Slovakian border, are the Tatra Mountains and the delightful ski resort town of Zakopane.

Cloth Hall, Kraków

To the southeast, between Kraków and Ukraine, is the 16th-century Renaissance town Zamość. Almost in the exact geographical centre of Poland is the present-day capital and commercial centre, Warsaw. Nearby is Lódz, Poland's second city. In north and northwest Poland are Gdańsk on the Baltic Sea, and nearby Malbork Castle, the most splendid fortification in Poland and the largest brick castle in the world. Toruń was the birthplace of the great Polish astronomer Copernicus, while Poznań is one of the most ancient centres in Poland and today one of its most dynamic cities.

## KRAKÓW

Elegant **Kraków**, the former royal capital of Poland, is one of the finest old cities in Europe. More than a thousand years old, and the country's capital for half that time, Kraków is Poland's third-largest city, with 750,000 people. It is also considered the heart and soul of Poland, home to many of its greatest artists, writers, musicians, filmmakers and one of the world's oldest universities. It is one of the few major towns in Poland not devastated by the world wars of the 20th century, and its miraculously preserved medieval market square and castle hill make it Poland's most seductive city.

### Adolf Hitler Platz

When Kraków was occupied by the Nazis, the Main Market Square was renamed Adolf Hitler Platz.

Though awe-inspiring churches, monuments and museums line its ancient streets, and the historic royal castle overlooks the Old Town from a hilltop, Kraków is one of Poland's liveliest and hippest cities. It abounds with young, fashionable café-hoppers. Kraków's roster of bars and cafés, many of them idiosyncratic places in underground cellars, are among the city's undeniable highlights. Almost everything of interest in Kraków is easily managed on foot, with the possible exception of Kazimierz, the old Jewish quarter that lies just south of the Old Town. Though a visitor could rush through Kraków and 'see' its Old Town and Wawel Hill in a couple of days, one would miss out on much of the alluring character of the city, which is best savoured over several days or a week.

## Main Market Square and Old Town

Kraków's layout dates from 1257 and remains almost unchanged to this day. The streets are lined with historic townhouses, fine churches and delightful small shops. The whole of the Old Town (Stare Miasto) is encircled by the **Planty**, a ring of relaxing parklands where massive fortifications and a wide moat once protected the city. The best place to begin to get to know Kraków is Europe's largest medieval **Market Square** (Rynek Główny), at the heart of the Old Town. The spectacular square pulsates with youthful energy at all hours,

Main Market Square

Under the Cloth Hall's arches

and its pavement cafés are fine places to enjoy the views of the square and the parade of Kraków's most fashionable denizens (and flight of the huge flock of pigeons). Many of the houses that line the square have Neo-Classical façades, though they are considerably older than that, and are full of interesting architectural details.

At the centre of the square is the **Cloth Hall** (Sukiennice), built in the 14th century and reconstructed after a fire in 1555 in the Renaissance style (the arcades were added in the 19th century). The building once housed the richest of Kraków's cloth merchants, and today its ground-floor stalls are occupied by privileged sellers of amber jewellery, religious artefacts, art and souvenirs targeting Kraków's year-round tourist trade. Indeed, the entire market square was once populated with merchants of all kinds, though today the only ones permitted are flower sellers and artists (as well as booths set up for special fairs).

Next to the Cloth Hall is the 15th-century **Town Hall Tower**; the rest of the Town Hall was demolished in the early 19th century. Southeast of it is tiny **St Adalbert's Church** (Kościół Św. Wojciecha). Intriguingly, the copper-domed 11th-century church is a couple of steps below the level of the square. The **Kraków Historical Museum** (Rynek Główny 35; open daily 10am–5.30pm; admission fee) in the former Krzysztofory Palace, contains a large collection of documents, paintings and model buildings attesting to the development of the city.

On the eastern side of the square, just beyond a statue of the 19th-century Romantic poet Adam Mickiewicz – a hangout for local youths and backpackers from around the globe – is **St Mary's Basilica** (Kościół Mariacki; open daily 11.30am–6pm; admission fee). The asymmetrical towers and turret-surrounded spire are one of Kraków's most celebrated images. A church from 1220 first stood on this spot, and it faced east, as was the custom of the day. St Mary's, built on the original foundations in the 14th century, also sits at an angle to the square.

The main entrance to St Mary's, a Baroque porch façade, is used only by those attending Mass. Tourists are asked to enter through the side door, along the passageway (St Mary's Square) off Rynek Główny. Inside is a stunning burst of ornamentation and colour, with extraordinary wall paintings by Jan Matejko in blue, green and pink. The ceiling of

St Mary's Basilica

the main nave is painted a bold blue with gold stars. The highlight, though, is the sumptuous altarpiece, a masterwork of Polish Gothic that took the 15th-century German artist Veit Stoss (Wit Stwosz) a dozen years to create, beneath five tall columns of stained-glass windows. The powerful altarpiece depicts the Dormition of the Virgin Mary, flanked by scenes of the life of Christ and the Virgin. Over the central nave is a massive crucifix; at the rear of the church is Art Nouveau stained glass, the work of Kraków's Stanisław Wyspiański, behind the organ loft.

The little courtyard south of St Mary's leads to **St Barbara's Church** (Kościół Św. Barbary) and a passageway onto **Little Market Square** (Mały Rynek), where colourful façades adorn what was once the site of meat, fish and poultry vendors (whose wares were moved from the Main Market Square due to their unpleasant odours).

One of the streets leading off the Main Market Square is ul. Floriańska, a busy pedestrian-only street full of shops, restaurants and cafés. On the eastern side is the **Jan Matejko House** (Dom Jana Matejki; open Tues–Wed and Sat–Sun 10am–7pm, Thur–Fri 10am–4pm; admission fee), the home where the 19th-century Polish master was born, worked and died. It includes memorabilia and a number of paintings from

## St Mary's Trumpeter

Every hour, a trumpeter appears in the high tower of St Mary's Basilica to play the Hejnał Mariacki, a call to arms that began as a warning of the advancing Tartar army in 1241. The tradition has been practised uninterrupted for several centuries. The bugle call ends mid-bar, a symbol of the story that the lone watchman was felled by an arrow as he warned the city. Watch the trumpeter from the passageway just south of the church; at the end of the piece, he waves to those gathered below.

The Barbican

his personal collection, and much of the house stands as the artist left it upon his death in 1893. At the end of the street, and the edge of the Old Town, is the **Floriańska Gate**, one of the original seven gates in the city's fortified walls. Built in 1300, it is the only one to have survived 19th-century modernisation plans. An outdoor art market is set up here daily, and pictures executed in every conceivable style blanket the stone walls. The view down Floriańska towards the spire of St Mary's is one of the most priceless in Kraków.

Just beyond the gate is the **Barbican** (Barbakan; open May–Oct daily 10.30am–6pm; admission fee), a circular brick bastion built at the end of the 15th century and one of the few remaining structures of the medieval fortifications. It was originally connected to the Floriańska Gate over a moat. Nearby are two buildings of significance. One is the **Church of the Holy Cross** (Kościół Św. Krzyża; pl. Św. Ducha), a small 15th-century church with splendid Gothic vaulting, and the other is the eclectic **Słowacki Theatre** (Teatr im. Juliusza Słowackiego; pl. Św. Ducha 1), a bright yellow-and-green-roofed structure built in 1893 and modelled after the Paris Opera House. Don't miss the curious laughing gargoyles on the rooftop.

At the top of ul. Św. Jana, the street running parallel and to the west of Floriańska, is one of the Old Town's highlights – the **Czartoryski Museum** (Muzeum Czartoryskich; ul. Św. Jana 19; open Wed and Fri–Sat 10am–6pm, Tues, Thur and Sun 10am–3.30pm; admission fee; <www.czartoryski.org>). This splendid museum in an immaculate palace contains a coveted portrait by Leonardo da Vinci *(Lady with an Ermine)*, one of just a handful of known oil portraits attributed to the great master and considered a worthy rival to the *Mona Lisa*. The stunning small painting, of a slender young woman with a bony hand stroking a curious little animal, was, no pun intended, repeatedly ferreted in and out of Poland to elude would-be thieves. In fact, the empty frame across the room from *Lady with an Ermine* is that of a Raphael portrait that didn't fare as well: it was stolen by the Nazis and never recovered. The museum also houses a great collection of Polish silver, early ecclesiastical relics from France, handsome groups of medieval religious art and military instruments, and an intriguing Rembrandt landscape, flush with minute detail and metaphorical meaning. Beyond the art works gathered is the intrinsic interest of visiting a palace belonging to one of Kraków's most prominent families, who were collectors on a grand scale.

The **Stanisław Wyspiański Museum** (Muzeum Stanisława Wyspiańskiego; ul. Szczepańska 11; open Tues and Thur–Fri 10am–3.30pm, Wed and Sat 10am–6pm; admission fee) features the art, design and writings of the Kraków artist. Wyspiański is perhaps best known for his stained glass and decorative frescoes (as seen in St Francis' Basilica; *see page 41*), but he was also a poet, designer and dramatist. This branch of the National Museum, in a 17th-century house, holds a large collection of Wyspiański's works, including architectural designs for civic buildings, stained-glass windows for churches, stage sets, portraits and landscapes.

The area south and west of the main market square is home to the famed **Jagiellonian University**, the oldest university in Poland and one of the oldest in Europe, and several fine churches. Take any of the streets heading west from the square, such as Św. Anny. Enter a small door beneath the Flemish-style roof to the **Collegium Maius** (ul. Jagiellońska 15; open Mon, Wed and Fri 10am–2.20pm, Tues and Thur 10am–5.20pm, Sat 10am–2pm; admission fee), the oldest building of the university and a beautiful 15th-century Gothic structure with an arcaded central courtyard. Be sure to see the fanciful drainage pipe heads, of medieval dragons and the like, on the rooftop. King Kazimierz established the uni-

Collegium Maius

**City of churches**

Kraków is said to have in excess of 125 churches – 60 of them in the Old Town alone.

versity in 1364, but its golden age dates to the period of the reign of King Jagiełło, for whom it is named. Copernicus allegedly studied here in the 16th century, and the guided visit inside to the University Museum – including ornate academic halls, the treasury, library and professors' dining hall – shows off several objects related to the university's most famous collegian and his theory that revolutionised our notion of the universe, including astronomical instruments, a registrar's book signed 'Mikołaj Kopernik', and a very rare globe, dating back to 1520, with the earliest known depiction of the Americas. Visits are conducted primarily in English, though the gentleman who generally leads the tours is conversant in several European languages. Pope John Paul II received an honorary doctorate at the university, and Poland's most recent Nobel Prize winner for literature, Wisława Szymborska, donated her medal and a good portion of the prize to the museum.

The streets near here are always filled with students – Kraków has nearly 100,000 students attending the university's 12 colleges and academic institutes. Around the corner from the Collegium Maius is **St Anne's Church** (Kościół Św. Anny; ul. Św. Anny 11), linked to the university and a favourite location for students getting married. The 17th-century interior is a superb example of airy Polish baroque, with a high dome, spectacular stucco work and wall murals. Facing the Planty is the **Collegium Novum**, a late 19th-century neo-Gothic building decorated with the crests of the university and its most celebrated benefactors. When Hitler's troops invaded Kraków in 1939, they stormed this hall and arrested nearly 200 professors and academics, and hauled them off to concentration camps.

On ul. Franciszkańska, directly south of the market square, is the unmissable **St Francis' Basilica** (Kościół Św. Franciszka z Asyżu; pl. Wszystkich Świętych), dating from 1269. The gutted interior was rebuilt in the 19th century after the last of four disastrous fires. Relatively unassuming from the exterior, the exuberant interior is a stunning assembly of brilliant stained glass and colourful wall paintings in floral and geometric motifs. At the rear above the organ loft is a remarkable Art Nouveau stained-glass window designed by the local artist Stanisław Wyspiański, a disciple of Jan Matejko, in 1900. The large 'Act of Creation' depicts God in wild streaks of colour. Wyspiański reportedly based God's face on the countenance of a beggar. The

stained-glass windows behind the altar, also by Wyspiański, depict the Blessed Salomea to the left and St Francis to the right. To the right of the altar is a passage to the Gothic cloister with its 15th-century frescoes and portraits of the bishops of Kraków. The painting at the end of the hall is of the 'lady who stopped the fire', a reference to the great fire of 1850 that was miraculously snuffed out at that very wall of the Franciscan church.

St Francis' Basilica

East of here the street changes name in honour of another religious order and its 13th-century church, the **Dominican Church and Monastery** (Kościół Dominikanów; ul. Stolarska 12). It too suffered from fire damage, and today is notable for its neo-Gothic chapels and original 15th-century portal. The monastery has serene Gothic cloisters.

Heading south towards Wawel Hill, along ul. Grodzka, is **SS Peter and Paul's Church** (Kościół Św. Piotra i Św. Pawła; ul. Grodzka 54), recognised by a large dome and long row of stately statues of the Twelve Apostles out front. The oldest Baroque building in Kraków, the basilica was founded by the Jesuits in the early 1600s. The rather austere late-Renaissance interior has recently been renovated.

The small Romanesque church next door is **St Andrew's** (Kościół Św. Andrzeja; ul. Grodzka 54), dating from the 11th

century and one of the oldest churches in Kraków. Its colourful history includes a stint as a hiding place and fortress for Poles battling invading Tartars in 1241.

Across the square facing those two churches, turn down ul. Kanonicza, one of Kraków's most attractive streets. On the way to Wawel Hill, at ul. Kanonicza 9, is the house where Stanisław Wyspiański lived and worked in the early 20th century.

Down the street, at ul. Kanonicza 19, is the **Archdiocesan Museum** (Muzeum Archidiecezjalne; ul. Kanonicza 19; open Tues–Fri 10am–4pm, Sat–Sun 10am–3pm; admission fee), where Pope John Paul II lived on two occasions, first as a young priest and then as Bishop of Kraków. The neighbouring 14th-century houses now contain a small museum of notable 13th- to 20th-century religious art, including a collection of Gothic sculptures of the Madonna and child, and artefacts belonging to the Pope, including the room where he lived (with his desk, bed and two pairs of skis), photographs, and ornate gifts from heads of state and religious leaders.

The other buildings on ul. Kanonicza are also worth a closer look, as many are former palaces with a range of architectural features, including Gothic, Renaissance and Baroque. Continuing along ul. Kanonicza, past the exclusive Hotel Copernicus, leads you towards Wawel Hill.

Sculptures in front of SS Peter and Paul's Church

## Wawel Hill

A castle or royal palace has existed on Wawel Hill overlooking the Old Town of Kraków since the 9th century, though the area may have been inhabited as early as the Paleolithic Age. The first kings of Poland maintained a royal residence here from the 10th century until King Zygmunt Waza (Sigismund Vasa) moved the royal seat to Warsaw in 1609. Over the centuries it was repeatedly destroyed by invaders and war, ultimately transformed into the complex that today is a mix of Gothic, Renaissance, Baroque and neo-Classical architecture.

Wawel, a symbol of the Polish nation, is a great source of national pride to Poles, and it is a popular place of spiritual pilgrimage. Principally visited are the royal castle and chambers, treasury and armoury, the cathedral and royal tombs, and Sigismund stairs to the bell tower. Expect crowds and large tour groups, especially in summer, and allow at least half a day for a full visit.

**Wawel Cathedral**

The Gothic edifice of **Wawel Cathedral** (Katedra; open Mon–Sat 9am–5pm, Sun 12.15–5pm; admission fee only for the crypt and bell tower) – what one sees today is the third cathedral built on this site – was begun in 1320, some three centuries after the first. The site of half a millennium of royal coronations and burials, it is the final resting place of nearly all the kings of Poland. The entrance is marked by a set of very large bones – those of a rhinoceros – that were found on the site and are said to protect the cathedral and all Kraków against those who would attempt to harm the city.

Bones marking the entrance to the cathedral

At the centre of the nave is an ornate **shrine to St Stanislaus**, the 13th-century bishop of Kraków who was martyred by the Polish king Bolesław in 1079. The saint's body was partitioned and, according to legend, it re-formed and became whole again – a sign taken as a portent that a divided Poland, partitioned by Germany, Russia and Austria, would also re-unify itself. The cathedral witnessed the coronation of 32 kings, each of whom knelt before the shrine and asked St Stanislaus for forgiveness. Of particular interest among the various tombs, altars and chapels is the highly ornamented, Renaissance-style **Sigismund Chapel**, designed by the Italian architect Bartolomeo Berrecci (it's the one with the gleaming golden dome seen from outside). To the right of the entrance, the **Holy Cross Chapel** is a feast of extraordinary 14th-century Byzantine frescoes and a late-15th-century marble sarcophagus. The chapel, the burial chamber of King Jagiełło, has been meticulously restored.

The tight, wooden 14th-century stairs leading to the **Sigismund Belltower** are not for the claustrophobic or disabled, but for the athletically inclined they're a fun climb up to see the revered Zygmunt bell, which dates to the mid-16th century and is the largest bell in Poland, requiring eight people

Stained-glass windows in Wawel Cathedral

to ring it. Krakovians say they can hear the bell from as far as 20km (12 miles) away when it is rung on major holidays.

Behind the altar is the tomb of Kazimierz the Great, the so-called 'Builder of Poland'. The mausoleums of the Sigismund kings, beloved Queen Jadwiga and others lie upstairs in the cathedral, while downstairs in the **Royal Crypts** are the tombs of 10 Polish kings and their families, as well as a handful of national military and literary heroes, including Marshall Piłsudski, who has a small and decidedly atmospheric crypt all to himself. The entrance to the tombs is towards the back of the church, and the exit is onto the main castle courtyard.

➤ **Wawel Castle**, also an enduring symbol of Polish nationhood, was the royal residence until 1609, when it was moved to Warsaw. King Bolesław built the first and considerably smaller residence in the 11th century, but it became a grand, Gothic palace during the reign of Kazimierz the Great in the 14th century. A great fire razed it in 1499, and the elegant Renaissance palace that was rebuilt by King Zygmunt is largely the structure one sees today. Swedes, Prussians and Austrians all overran and occupied the castle and its grounds, and the last group of invaders destroyed churches and built military barracks, leaving the hill with an oddly empty square and large and plainer buildings to the west of the castle. The Polish government and people did not recover Wawel until the end of World War I in 1918, when the partition of Poland ended. Visits are restricted to certain sections of the castle. Purchase tickets in the passageway between the cathedral and castle.

The **State Rooms** and **Royal Private Apartments** (Reprezentacyjne Komnaty Królewskie and Prywatne Apartamenty Królewskie; open Tues–Sat 9.30am–4pm; admission fee) are the largest and most interesting part of the castle. They have been nicely restored to their original Renaissance style and furnished with Baroque and Renaissance furniture, much of which is not original but certainly representative of royal lifestyle. The most impressive and valuable items on display are without doubt the spectacular collection of 16th-century Flemish tapestries commissioned by King Sigismund. Only 136 of the original 364 tapestries (all ordered at the same time) survive, and not all are on view. The tapestries have a particularly peripatetic history. At various times, many were stolen and others taken

## Ticket tips

Separate tickets are needed for the cathedral and castle complexes. Guided group visits are available at the main box office past the cathedral (there are two other box offices, including one on the path on the way up the hill). The various component parts of Wawel have different opening hours, so be sure to check them before visiting. For the latest information, check the official Wawel website at <www.wawel.krakow.pl>.

Throne and tapestries in Wawel Castle

out of the country for safekeeping. After World War II, they travelled from Romania to France and England and finally Canada before being recovered for Poland in 1968.

Also on view is a handsome collection of 17th-century Turkish tents in an exhibition of Oriental art.

The **Deputies Hall**, or Throne Room, is also called the 'Heads Room', a name that is explained once you glance at the ceiling. It is festooned with small carved wooden heads of some 30 citizens of Renaissance-period Kraków – ordinary folk, not just royalty, nobles and clergy as might be expected. Over the king's throne is a stunning Flemish tapestry. The **Senators' Room** is wall-to-wall with tapestries placed over the windows, reportedly so there would be no outside distractions during important Senate sessions. It is the only room where the original placement of tapestries is known.

The **Treasury and Armoury** (Skarbiec Koronny i Zbrojownia; open Tues–Sat 9.30am–4pm, Sun 10am–4pm; admission fee), in vaulted Gothic rooms that were part of the 14th-century castle, house the royal collection of weaponry and spoils of war, including a Royal Jagged Sword present at all Polish coronations from the early 14th century on. As if that's not enough, at the foot of the hill, Wawel also has a **Dragon's Cave** (open May–Nov daily 10am–6pm; admission fee), according to legend the home of a reclusive dragon, *Smok Wawelski*. After descending into the cave, you emerge on the banks of the Vistula River.

## Kazimierz

Home to an old Jewish district of Kraków, **Kazimierz** was originally built in 1335 as an independent, planned and walled town by the Polish king whose name it took. Jews, persecuted throughout Europe, were offered refuge in Kraków, but King Jan Olbracht moved Kraków's entire Jewish population to Kazimierz at the end of the 15th century. Today the district is essentially a suburb within easy walking distance or a short tram or taxi ride from the Old Town.

Before the war, some 60,000 Jews lived in the Kraków area. Only a few thousand remained in 1945, and today there are reportedly as few as 200 here. After decades of neglect, having been robbed of its people and soul – although many of its buildings survived the war – Kazimierz is undergoing a revitalisation. Jewish foundations from around the world are funding the restoration of historic buildings, and Steven Spielberg brought new attention to Kazimierz with his Academy Award-winning 1994 film *Schindler's List*, much of which was filmed in the area. As visitors to Kraków discover Kazimierz, new hotels, cafés and restaurants are moving in, and there are signs that young Krakovians now see it as more than the devastating reminder of a tragic period in Polish history. Some Jews are even beginning to return and attempt to reclaim their property.

Commemorating Jewish history

The easiest way to get to Kazimierz is to take the blue express tram No. 3 south from the Planty just outside Old Town and get off at the third stop along ul. Starowiślna. If walking from Wawel Hill, take ul. Stradomska (which becomes ul. Krakowska) south and turn left at ul. Józefa.

Among dilapidated buildings and new businesses in the Jewish quarter are many signs and insignias of the Jewish population. Eight synagogues (of the 30 that once existed here) survived the war, of which a couple have been established as museums. Ul. Szeroka, which means Wide Street but is actually more of a square, was the heart of the district from the 15th century onwards. On the west side of the square is the **Remu'h Synagogue and Cemetery** (ul. Szeroka 40; open Sun–Fri 9am–6pm; admission fee), a small 500-year-old synagogue that remains in use. The second-oldest in the district, it is perhaps the most important synagogue in the area today. Jews visit to touch the chair of the 16th-century Rabbi Moses Isserles, a great philosopher and lawyer, and a black feast calendar is one of the few surviving elements of the original synagogue. Much of the cemetery next door was destroyed by the Nazis, though several hundred gravestones, many of them 400 years old and buried by the Jews themselves to avoid desecration by invaders of the 18th century, were discovered during excavations after the war. The handful of tombs enclosed by a fence includes that of Rabbi Isserles, which is often covered with small stones, measures of respect left behind by Jewish visitors. Legend holds that the Nazis were in the process of levelling the rabbi's grave along with all the others when one of the workers was felled by a heart attack. The Wailing Wall at one end of the cemetery is made up of fragments of gravestones that were destroyed by the Germans.

At the south end of ul. Szeroka is the **Old Synagogue** (ul. Szeroka 24; open Mon and Wed–Thur 10am–4pm, Fri 10am–5pm; admission fee). Dating from the 15th century, it is the oldest surviving Jewish house of worship in Poland. Today it houses a museum of Jewish history and culture, with an ornate 16th-century wrought-iron *bimah*, or pulpit, in the centre of the main prayer hall. Upstairs, an exhibition of Nazi newspapers and photographs depicts war-time experiences in Kazimierz.

Old Synagogue

One street to the west is the large **Isaac Synagogue** (ul. Kupa 18; open Mon–Sat 9am–7pm; admission fee), a cavernous hall that was once the most beautiful of all the synagogues here, with opulent Baroque stucco decoration from the mid-17th century that was destroyed by the Nazis. Today, at the end of the otherwise empty room, school groups and other visitors sit silently in front of televisions and watch a sombre documentary of Jewish life *(The Memory of Polish Jews)* set to plaintive music that evokes the Holocaust. Next to the synagogue is an atmospheric, bohemian café, **Singer**, where some of the tables are old Singer sewing machine stands.

The **Jewish Cultural Centre** (ul. Rabina Meiselsa 17; open Mon–Fri 10am–6pm, Sat–Sun 10am–2pm; <www.judaica. pl>) is located just west of pl. Nowy, the old Jewish marketplace. It has regular exhibitions and conferences aimed at preserving knowledge of Jewish culture. A superb photographic exhibition of Jewish heritage can be seen at the **Galicia Jewish Museum** (ul. Dajwór 18; open daily 9am–7pm; admission fee; <www.galiciajewishmuseum.org>).

Western Kazimierz is the Catholic section of the planned town and is marked by three churches: **Corpus Christi** Church (Kościół Bozego Ciala; ul. Bozego Ciala 15), the Gothic **St Catherine's Church** (Kościół Św. Katarzyny; ul. Augustiańska 7) and the **Pauline Church** (Kościół Paulinów; ul. Skałeczna). Celebrated cultural figures, including Stanisław Wyspiański, are buried in the crypt of the latter, where it is also said that Kraków's St Adalbert was mutilated and then miraculously resurrected. On pl. Wolnica is the old town hall, which now houses an **Ethnographic Museum** (Muzeum Etnograficzne; pl. Wolnica 1; open Mon 10am–6pm, Wed–Fri 10am–3pm, Sat–Sun 10am–2pm; admission fee),

New Cemetery

said to be the largest in the country, with exhibits that depict the region's rural and folk traditions.

The **New Jewish Cemetery** (Nowy Cmentarz Żydowski; ul. Miodowa 55; open Sun–Fri 10am–dusk), a short walk northeast of ul. Szeroka, is a large, haunted-looking place of toppled gravestones with Yiddish insignias and lettering grown over by bright green moss. The cemetery was founded in 1800 and, though appearing wholly abandoned today, is the only current burial place for Jews in Kraków.

> **Jewish culture**
>
> Now running for over 20 years, the annual Jewish Festival of Culture is a great way to discover both Kraków's Jewish past and the vibrant Jewish culture that remains in the city. Highlights of the 10-day festival include kosher cooking, Hassidic dancing and some of the best Klezmer music you'll hear. For more information, see <www.jewishfestival.pl>.

The actual ghetto where the Nazis forced the Jews to live between 1941 and 1943 is located across the river over Powstańców bridge at the end of ul. Starowiślna, in the Podgórze district. Here you'll find another place of interest and pilgrimage, the **Museum of National Remembrance** (Muzeum Pamięci Narodowej; pl. Bohaterów Getta 18; open Tues–Thur and Sat 9.30am–4pm, Fri 10am–5pm; admission fee), better known as the Pharmacy Under the Eagle (Apteka pod Orłem). Now a small museum of Jewish life in the ghetto, it was once a pharmacy belonging to a Pole – the only Gentile whom the Germans allowed to live in the ghetto – who witnessed the murders of 1,000 Jews and decided to give shelter to as many as he could. Tadeusz Pankiewicz later was one of the critical witnesses at the Nuremberg trials. Nearby, off ul. Lwowska to the southwest of the pharmacy, is a still-standing section of the wall that the Nazis constructed around the ghetto. If the top of the wall looks familiar, it

## In the ghetto

Jews in the war-time ghetto were required by the Nazis to: have a Star of David designating all businesses; carry Jewish identity cards at all times; and ride on the back half of trams, which were labelled *Für Juden* (for Jews).

is because Hitler's agents designed the wall to mimic the form of traditional Jewish gravestones, the message delivered a clear 'here is where you shall die'. Oskar Schindler's former Emalia enamel factory still stands at the edge of Podgórze, on ul. Lipowa.

Most visitors to Kraków stick to the Old Town and Wawel Hill, and perhaps Kazimierz and separate trips to Auschwitz and the Wieliczka Salt Mines *(see opposite)*. If you have more time, though, just west of the Old Town is the **National Museum** (Muzeum Narodowe; al. 3 Maja 1; open Tues and Thur 10am–4pm, Wed and Fri–Sat 10am–7pm, Sun 10am–3pm; admission fee; <www.muzeum. krakow.pl>). The off-putting, Soviet-style architecture gives way to an important collection including 14th-century stained glass and decorative arts, furniture and vestments from Wawel, a wonderful collection of paintings, sculptures and other works by leading 20th-century Polish artists and a wide array of military armaments and uniforms, of great interest to history enthusiasts. It also hosts most of the important touring exhibitions that come to Kraków.

Those interested in architecture and Japanese culture should visit the **Manggha** (ul. Konopnickiej 26; open Tues–Sun 10am–6pm; admission fee; <www.manggha.krakow.pl>), a centre of Japanese art and technology, across the river south of Wawel Hill and west of Kazimierz. The splendid futuristic building, by the Japanese architect Arata Isozaki, holds a collection of Samurai armour, pottery and woodblock prints. One of Poland's most famous film directors, Andrzej Wajda, won the Kyoto prize and donated his prize money to found the centre.

# EXCURSIONS FROM KRAKÓW

## Wieliczka Salt Mines

**Wieliczka** (ul. Daniłowicza 10, Wieliczka; open daily
7.30am–7.30pm; admission fee; <www.kopalnia.pl>, <www.
muzeum.wieliczka.pl>), a series of deep mines more than 700
years old located about 15km (9 miles) southeast of Kraków,
makes for an extraordinary subterranean adventure. The
mine reaches 327m (1,073ft) and nine levels underground.
Visitors descend 378 steps down to the first level of 64m
(210ft) and then pass through 3km (2 miles) of tunnels, visiting some 20 chambers and chapels carved out of salt by
miners. The St Anthony Chapel dates to 1698. But the largest
and most astounding chapel is the **Chapel of the Blessed
St Kinga**. Everything in it is carved out of salt. Its chandeliers, altar and remarkable relief carving (with great per-

Inside the Salt Mine

spective) of the Last Supper were created over a period of 70 years, beginning in the 19th century, by just three miners, who were obviously talented and dedicated sculptors (like all the chapels and chambers, this massive hall was carved in the miners' time off). Weddings are occasionally held in the St Kinga Chapel, as is Mass three times a year. Along the way in other chambers you'll also see green-salt statues of Copernicus and even, curiously, the Seven Dwarves.

Protected by UNESCO as a World Heritage Site, the mine was the property of the Polish Royal Family (for whom the salt, called 'grey gold', contributed one-third of the total royal wealth) until the 1772 partition of Poland, when it fell to the Austrians. Salt mining continued here until 1996, and today the mine is visited by tour groups and those seeking relief from respiratory ailments like asthma in the sanatorium 200m (656ft) below the ground. During World War II,

Monument to the salt workers

the Nazis used the tallest chamber (which measures 36m/118ft from floor to ceiling) as a secret factory for the manufacture of aircraft parts, staffed by Jewish prisoners. A few years back, a couple of thrillseekers pulled off a bungee jump and others conducted the first underground balloon flight, documented by the *Guinness Book of World Records*, in the same chamber. During July and August, a miners' orchestra plays in the lake chamber, treating visitors to a 170-year-old tradition.

At the end of the two-hour visit to the mine, you can either visit the museum of mining equipment and geological specimens (separate ticket required) or be whisked back to ground level by a wooden elevator.

Visitors to Wieliczka must be accompanied by guides. Individuals can join tour groups with commentaries in either Polish or English (if there is none in English, purchase an English-language guide and tag along behind a Polish group). To get to Wieliczka, the cheapest and most efficient means is to take a contra-bus marked Wieliczka–Kraków at the train station in Kraków. It is a good idea to book guides in advance in summer when groups can overrun the mine.

## Auschwitz and Birkenau

Poland was ground zero for Nazi Germany's terrible campaign to rid the world of all Jews, and Auschwitz concentration camp was one of the most efficient elements in their killing machine. Visiting it and the neighbouring Birkenau camp is a chilling and unforgettable experience. Both Auschwitz (or Auschwitz I to give it its proper name) and Birkenau (Auschwitz II) are in the town of Oświęcim (Auschwitz being the Germanised version of the name), 75km (47 miles) west of Kraków.

At Birkenau, an inscription bluntly reads: 'Forever let this place be a cry of despair and a warning to Humanity, where the Nazis murdered about one and a half million men, women, and children, mainly Jews from various countries of Europe.' The horrors of the acts that were carried out here, and the reality of lost lives and potential, are unfathomable.

**Auschwitz** (open daily 8am–7pm; free; <www.auschwitz. org.pl>) was originally a Polish army barracks. Jews from as far away as Norway and Greece were loaded into wretched, sealed trains with no water, food or bathrooms, and very little air to breathe, and herded to the concentration camps in Poland. The first 728 'prisoners of war', most of them Polish and all of them from the town of Tarnów, were brought here in June 1940. After that, streams of Jews, as well as Soviet prisoners, were relocated to the camps. They became slave labourers; many died of starvation, while some were summarily executed and many others were herded into gas chambers and killed with lethal Zyklon B gas.

A short and disturbing documentary film is shown in English, German and French at regular intervals. It features orig-

## Oskar Schindler

Immortalised first in Thomas Keneally's book *Schindler's Ark* and later in the Oscar-winning film *Schindler's List*, directed by Steven Spielberg, the enigmatic German businessman Oskar Schindler (1908–74) lived and worked in Kraków during World War II. He bought a bankrupt enamel factory in Podgórze and employed cheap Jewish labour, saving thousands of lives by bribing and hoodwinking scores of high-ranking Nazis throughout the war. His famous list dates from the summer of 1944, and was made up of 1,100 Jewish men, women and children destined for the gas chambers at Auschwitz whom he saved by sending to another factory he owned in what is now the Czech Republic. After his death Schindler was buried on Jerusalem's Mount Zion, recognised as one of the Righteous Among Nations.

inal footage, shot by the Soviet troops who liberated the camp in 1945, and is a good, if startling, introduction for trying to comprehend what you're about to see. After viewing the film, pass under the famous gates of entry to Auschwitz, which are inscribed with the cruel slogan *Arbeit Macht Frei* (Work Makes Free).

About 30 cell blocks, as well as watchtowers and barbed-wire fences, survived the Nazi attempt to destroy the camp when they fled at the conclusion of the war. You can walk freely among the blocks and enter those that are open. In one, behind glass cases you'll see collections of piles of shoes, twisted spectacles, tons of human hair, and suitcases with the names and addresses of prisoners – who were told they were simply being relocated to a new town – stencilled on them. Hallways are lined with rows of mug shots of the prisoners, some adorned with flowers from surviving family members. Outside Block 11, the so-called 'Block of Death', is an execution wall where prisoners were shot. Inside is where the Nazis carried out their first experiments gassing prisoners with Zyklon B. Another barrack nearby is dedicated to the 'Martyrdom of the Jewish People'. At the end of the exhibit of

Grim sight: lookout tower and barbed wire, Auschwitz

### Getting there

To get to Auschwitz, you can take a 2-hour train or frequent bus (90 minutes; Nos 2–5 or 24–30) leaving from in front of Kraków's train station. However, you will need to take a taxi or walk to Birkenau from Auschwitz, as there is no frequent bus service. Alternatively, you could sign up for one of the many package tours offered by any travel agency in Kraków.

historical documents and photographs, a haunting and mournful soundtrack, the song *Oh God the Merciful*, plays while the names of people killed at death camps are read.

**Birkenau** (open daily 8am–7pm; free), about 3km (2 miles) from Auschwitz, was built in 1941 when Hitler went beyond simply collecting political prisoners and embarked on a mass extermination programme. Its 300 long barracks on 175 hectares (523 acres) served as holding cells for the most murderous machinery of Hitler's extermination 'solution' for the Jews. Approximately three-quarters of all the Jews deported to Birkenau were gassed upon arrival. Indeed, Birkenau was the very definition of a death camp: it had its own railway station for transporting prisoners, four huge gas chambers, each of which was capable of gassing 2,000 prisoners at a time, and crematoria were outfitted with electric lifts to take the bodies to the ovens.

Visitors can climb to the second storey of the principal watchtower at the entrance, from where it is apparent just how vast this camp was. Stretching out are seemingly unending lines of barracks, watchtowers and barbed-wire fences; the camp could hold a total of 200,000 inmates. At the rear of the camp, beyond a grisly pond where the ashes of the murdered were dumped, is an enigmatic monument to the dead of the Holocaust, with inscriptions in the 20 languages of the prisoners who were murdered at Auschwitz and Birkenau.

# ZAKOPANE AND THE TATRA MOUNTAINS

Europe's second-largest chain of mountains after the Alps, the Carpathian Mountains *(Karpaty)* along the southern border of Poland, are where many Poles go to relax. It is a beautiful area of forests, lakes, historic mountain towns and spa villages, with great hiking and skiing. The High Tatras are the highest range of the Carpathians, and the most attractive town is Zakopane, nearly on the border with Slovakia and Poland's unofficial winter capital. A 2-hour drive south of Kraków, it is easily reached by buses that leave frequently from Kraków's main PKS bus station; trains are considerably slower (4 hours).

## Zakopane
A small, Alpine-like village, **Zakopane** is undeniably appealing, with a terrific backdrop of snow-capped moun-

Spectacular views near Zakopane

Traditional Zakopane costume

tains and wooden chalets built in the distinctive local, so-called Zakopane Style. A remote mountain outpost until it began to gain notice in the late 1800s, Zakopane is popular for both winter and summer holidays, drawing each year more than two million visitors, who come here for outdoor sports and shopping opportunities. It is also a centre of *Górale* (mountain people) folk art, traditional mountain music, and a unique style of wooden highlander architecture that was elevated to high art in the mid-19th century by several notable artists and architects.

The village's main drag is the pedestrian-only shopping street **ul. Krupówki**, where fashionable visitors parade up and down day and night. There are several interesting wooden buildings, horse carriages for hire, and sellers of folk art and local snacks. At the lower end of the promenade, the **Tatra Museum** (Muzeum Tatrzańskie; ul. Krupówki 10; open Wed–Sat 9am–4.30pm, Sun 9am–3pm; admission fee) houses a collection of local folk art and exhibits on local flora and fauna.

At the end of ul. Krupówki, turn left at ul. Kościeliska. 200m (650ft) or so on the right side is the old parish **St Mary of Częstochowa Church** (Kościół Matki Boskiej Częstochowskiej; ul. Kościeliska 4; open daily 9.30am–6pm), a splendid, tiny rustic wooden chapel dating from 1847. Next to it is an old cemetery, **Stary Cmentarz**, populated with a fascinating array of carved wooden tombstones and grave-markers, demonstrating the predominant mountain artistry that is often highly creative. The wooden homes nearby are excellent examples of the Zakopane Style.

Zakopane has earned a reputation as an artists' village, and there are several galleries and small museums of interest. One is the **Władysław Hasior Gallery** (Galeria Władysława Hasiora; ul. Jagiellońska 18b; open Wed–Sat 11am–6pm, Sun 9am–3pm; admission fee). Located close to the train station, it shows the works of the artist Władysław Hasior (1928–99), who was closely associated with Zakopane.

## The Tatras

At the foot of the **Tatras**, Zakopane is blessed with one of the most spectacular landscapes in Poland. Even if you haven't come to ski, it's fun and worthwhile to take the cable car up to **Mt Kasprowy** for the splendid views of the mountains, hiking trails and ski slopes above the town. The cable car ride,

### Witkacy

Warsaw-born Stanisław Ignacy Witkiewicz (1885–1939), aka Witkacy, was a gifted and eccentric painter, photographer and playwright whose strange life is part of Zakopane legend. Accused of murdering his fiancée in 1914, Witkacy set off on a voyage of discovery that took him to Australia, from where he returned to fight the Germans, create some puzzling, drug-induced work, descend into bouts of depression and start a theatre company in Zakopane that still bears his name. Witkacy took his own life when the Red Army invaded Poland on 17 October 1939 and was buried first in a remote part of Ukraine before being returned to Zakopane in 1988. In one final Witkacy-style twist, the wrong body was returned and his corpse has been lost for all eternity.

Snowy hike in the Tatras

about 25 minutes long with a stop and transfer at an intermediate station, takes you (and crowds of skiers in winter) up to the summit of Mt Kasprowy Wierch, at 1,985m (6512ft). There you can stand with one foot in Poland, the other in Slovakia. Reasonably priced return cable car tickets give you a mandatory 100 minutes at the top, so if you don't have skis or don't plan to hike, you might want to bring a book. In summer, many people take the ride up and walk back down along a series of marked trails (about 2 hours). To get to the cable car station in Kuźnice (south of Zakopane), take a taxi, bus No. 7 from directly in front of the bus station, or a minibus across the street from the bus stop.

If you're interested in hiking excursions in the area, including everything from easy walks through valleys to hardcore Tatra excursions to beautiful lakes, enquire at the rustic-looking tourism office (ul. Kościuszki 17; open daily 8am–6pm), near the bus station. The Tatras are for serious mountaineers only, and require special equipment and a guide. Less taxing nature spots suitable for day-long hiking include the valleys Dolina Białego, Dolina Strążyska, Dolina Chochołowska and Dolina Kościeliska.

The International Festival of Highland Culture is held every August in Zakopane. Essentially a week-long mountain folklore contest and full schedule of concerts, music competitions and parades, it has been held since 1968, and is an excellent introduction to the unique mountain culture of the Górale people.

## MAŁOPOLSKA

Małopolska, or Little Poland, occupies the southeast corner of the country between Kraków and Ukraine. The small and agreeably sleepy town of **Sandomierz** is a handsome former trading port on the banks of the Vistula. One of Poland's most ancient towns, it prospered during the Renaissance. Its old town, on a hill above the river, has a smattering of fine buildings, including the town hall on the Rynek, or market square, a 14th-century cathedral and castle, and St James's Church, built in 1230. Of particular interest to visitors is the underground route that dips into a couple of dozen cellars beneath the townhouses on the Rynek.

The banks of the Vistula

### Zamość

The small Renaissance town of **Zamość** is one of Poland's little gems. The Old Town has more than 100 buildings and monuments of artistic and historic distinction. The city was planned by the politician and nobleman Jan Zamoyski (1542–1605), who sought to build a perfect city, enclosed within fortifications, in the centre of the Lublin Upland. To carry out his plan, Zamoyski commissioned an Italian architect from Padua, Bernardo Morando, in 1580. The town's strategic location on important East–West trade routes resulted in considerable prosperity in the 17th century. Its fortifications were so strong that it was impregnable to the Tartars and Cossacks in the early 17th century, and was one of only three cities in Poland able to resist the Swedish Deluge of 1656.

Zamość's **Market Square** (Rynek), dominated by a large, pink town hall with a tall Baroque clock tower, is one of Poland's most splendid. To the right of the town hall are richly ornamented and arcaded houses painted vivid green, yellow, brick-red and blue, with Oriental detailing of 17th-century Armenian merchants. The other houses on the remaining three sides of the square are plainer and painted

in more subtle pastels, but don't detract from the square's great harmony. On each side of the Rynek are eight houses (save the north side, which is dominated by the town hall).

On the north side of the Rynek is the **Regional Museum** (Muzeum Okręgowe; ul. Ormiańska 30; open Tues–Sun 9am–6pm; admission fee), which houses an array of items ranging from archaeological finds to armaments and religious sculptures, including an interesting clay model of the Zamość Old Town and paintings of the Zamoyski clan. More importantly, the museum is an opportunity to walk through the interior of two of the grand old burgher houses on the Rynek. Much of the houses' rich detailing – stone

carving, frescoes around the top of rooms, and handsome wood-beam ceilings – have been well restored.

Just north of the Rynek is the former Jewish Quarter. In its heyday, Zamość was a multicultural city; Jews, Armenians, Germans, Greeks, Turks, Dutch and Italians all came to the city to trade. The former synagogue here now houses the town library.

West of the Rynek is the large but rather plain **Lord's Resurrection and St Thomas the Apostle Cathedral** (Katedra pw. Zmartwychwstania Pańskiego i Św. Tomaśza Apostoła; ul. Kolegiacka 2). To its immediate south, the **Religious Museum** (Muzeum Sakralne Kolegiaty Zamojskiej; ul. Kolegiacka 1a;

Market Square, Zamość

open Mon–Fri 10am–4pm, Sat–Sun 10am–1pm; admission fee) is a small, three-room collection of mostly Renaissance religious objects and paintings with curious translations into English like 'fourth heir in tail'.

On the eastern edge of the Old Town is the one surviving bastion of the seven that once formed the massive fortifications surrounding Zamość. The **Lviv Gate** (Brama Lwowska), next to a large and rather uninteresting market, is one of three original entrances to the city. Across from it is the large **Franciscan Church** (Kościół Franciszkanów), which retains none of its Baroque splendour, as it was destroyed when occupiers transformed it into a hospital and then military barracks. Today it is little more than a barren shell, though it still fills up for Mass.

Even though Zamość is a UNESCO World Heritage Site, its citizens don't yet seem quite accustomed to the curious attentions and cameras of foreign tourists in their midst. That makes it a good place to see a very pretty and exceedingly well-preserved little town where the citizens don't yet all speak English, and go about their business with little regard for the *złoty* of outsiders. On the other hand, if you're looking for something to do after taking in the main square and handful of streets that define Zamość's relaxed Old Town, you might be better off moving on to Kraków or Warsaw. If that's the case, there are regular bus and train services that take about 5–6 hours to either destination, though the connections from Lublin are faster and more frequent.

Lush countryside around Lublin

Castle walls and Vistula River, Kazimierz Dolny

## Kazimierz Dolny

The small, charming mercantile town **Kazimierz Dolny**, perched on the banks of the Vistula, became wealthy from the grain trade in the 16th century. Kazimierz has become a popular day-trip from Warsaw, and is likely to be busy on summer weekends.

The Old Town is notable for several fine burgher's town houses with elaborate Renaissance stucco work around the Rynek, or Market Square, which is also distinguished by a central wooden well. A couple of small museums – the Goldsmith Museum and the fine Celejowska House telling the story of the town – are also worth exploring.

The ruins of the town's 14th-century castle, a short walk north of the Rynek, provide good views above the river, though they're better at the watchtower a little further up the hill and best at Three Crosses Hilltop, a steep climb east of the Rynek. You can reach it returning from the watchtower.

## WARSAW

King Sigismund Vasa moved the royal court from the ancient city of Kraków to **Warsaw**, on the banks of the River Vistula in the centre of the country, in 1609. Though Kraków would remain the cultural and spiritual heart of Poland, the new political and administrative centre in Warsaw grew rapidly, adding wide boulevards and palatial residences to the small Old and New Towns.

Over the centuries, the city suffered from repeated invasions, occupations and destruction and had to be rebuilt on several occasions. World War II proved to be far more devastating and tragic than any of the previous conflicts; towards the end of the war, with the Soviet Red Army advancing inexorably, Hitler gave orders for the entire city to be systematically destroyed, and Warsaw was almost entirely levelled.

The rooftops of Warsaw's Old Town

Miraculously, the Old Town was later studiously rebuilt, although not exactly as it was, according to old photographs, paintings and architectural plans.

Though Warsaw is the nation's capital, it usually proves less captivating to visitors than Kraków or Gdańsk. In part, this is because it is still a city in transition, leading the way for the new post-Communist Poland – Poland as a member of NATO and the European Union. Outside the Old Town, the city can be unattractive – the architecture a haphazard and sometimes ugly mix of Stalinist concrete tower blocks, older buildings in need of restoration, and gleaming modern towers, all constructed with little thought given to urban

Warsaw's New Town

planning. Neighbourhoods are somewhat difficult to define. Still, it's a dynamic city of two million people with an important Royal Way, stunningly rejuvenated historic centre, reminders of the Warsaw Ghetto and monuments of Jewish legacy, and an important cultural nucleus.

The Vistula divides Warsaw down the middle, but almost everything of interest to visitors is located on the west bank. The Royal Way, the focus of most sightseeing, stretches from the Old Town south to Łazienki Park and Wilanów, formerly a royal summer palace.

## The Old Town and Market Square

Warsaw's **Old Town** (Stare Miasto) would be remarkable even if it hadn't been rebuilt from scratch after being razed during World War II. How extensive was the annihilation? Some historians estimate that 85 percent of the Old Town was destroyed. It is impossible not to marvel that within a period of around 30 years from the war's end, the entire Old Town was resurrected with abundant care for the architecture, aesthetics and soul of Warsaw. Competition for rebuilding projects was intense, and in fact, many other towns were neglected because of the resources directed to Warsaw. Incredibly, it looks, and more importantly feels, authentic, like a town with a medieval layout and Renaissance façades. The reconstructed town is a true testament to a people who refused to be defeated, even though the city's population had been reduced by more than two-thirds. Although some of the buildings only date from the mid-1950s, the Old Town was added in its entirety to UNESCO's list of World Heritage Sites in 1980.

It's probably best to begin a tour of Warsaw at the entrance to the Old Town, **Castle Square** (Plac Zamkowy). A tall column with a bronze **statue of King Sigismund** – who moved the capital to Warsaw – marks the square, against a backdrop of vibrantly coloured pastel town houses with red tile roofs. The fortifications that once enclosed the Old Town were dismantled in the 19th century, though you can still see frag-

The Royal Castle

ments of them on one side of the square. On the eastern side of the square is the massive **Royal Castle** (Zamek Królewski; pl. Zamkowy 4; open Mon–Sat 10am–4pm, Sun 11am–4pm; admission fee). Although a fortress was first established on this spot in the 1300s, the present structure is, like the whole of its surroundings, a recent 20th-century reconstruction.

> ### Fireman's Museum
>
> A fun and free thing to do with the children is to visit Warsaw's fabulous **Fireman's Museum** (Muzeum Historii i Techniki Pożarniczej; ul. Chłodna 3; open Mon–Fri 9am–2pm). The door is always locked, so visitors must ring the bell. A free pamphlet in English is available inside the museum.

In 1944, it was little more than a smoking pile of rubble, with all its great interiors destroyed by bullets, dynamite and fire. Almost all the royal collection of great works of art and tapestries was stolen or destroyed, though it should be noted that many pieces, including furnishings, were removed for safe-keeping when the war broke out. Reconstruction did not begin until 1971, and the Castle was reopened to the public in 1984.

As visitors to the castle pass through the stately rooms with excellent stucco detailing and lush works of art (some of which are copies of originals), they have to keep reminding themselves of the fact that what they are seeing was rebuilt in its entirety in the past 30 years. Fragments of original building materials, including decorative carvings and elements of stucco, were used in every possible case, and, if you look hard enough, you may be able to distinguish what is new from what is original.

The Royal Castle was the official residence of the kings of Poland from the 17th century onwards, and it is where Poland's landmark Constitution – the second oldest in the world, after that of the United States – was passed by the Sejm (parliament) on 3 May 1791. The Castle interior is visited according to two routes, for which there is nor-

### Sunday best

Sunday visits to the Royal Castle, from 11am–4pm, feature a single route that includes the most attractive parts of Routes I and II. Even better, the visit is free on Sunday. Guided visits for groups (extra charge) are available every day but Sunday.

mally separate admission. Route I takes in the ground-level courtiers' lodgings, parliamentary chambers, Prince Stanisław's apartment and the Jan Matejko rooms. Route II visits the upper-level Great and King's apartments. Each tour is estimated to take about an hour. If you have limited time and can follow only one route, you should probably opt for Route II, which covers the true highlights of the Castle.

The **King Stanisław August apartments** are among the most opulent rooms in the castle. On the upper level, the massive, mid-18th-century Ballroom – used variously as a concert hall, meeting and audience room, and the first room to be destroyed in 1939 – is perhaps the most stunning of all the rooms. Note the aptly named ceiling painting (a reconstruction), *The Dissolution of Chaos*.

The **Canalletto Room** showcases detailed paintings of Warsaw's Old Town architecture, by the Italian Bernardo Bellotto; these paintings survived the war and were instrumental in the capital's reconstruction efforts. In the **Marble Room**, another highlight, you'll see portraits of the 22 kings of Poland. The **Throne Room** glitters with a red-and-gold canopy of handmade silver-embroidered eagles. The originals were stolen by the Germans, but one eagle was recovered in the United States in 1991. It was bought by the Castle, and from it the entire canopy was reconstructed.

You can also visit the **Castle Cellars**, where a fascinating exhibition of remnants recovered from excavations in the Old Town is displayed (accessible with any ticket).

From **Plac Zamkowy**, head north along ul. Świętojańska. On the right is St John's Cathedral (Archikatedra Św. Jana), the oldest in Warsaw, dating from the 14th century. The cathedral was largely levelled during the war; though the Gothic brick exterior was rebuilt, too much of the interior was lost, and the Cathedral now looks wholly different from when the last king of Poland, Stanisław August Poniatowski, was crowned and buried here. The crypt holds the tombs of several famous Poles, among them the dukes of Mazovia, the Nobel Prize-winning writer Henryk Sienkiewicz, and first president of Poland, Gabriel Narutowicz. St John's played a role during the 1944 Warsaw Uprising against the German occupiers. German tanks even entered the confines of the church. If you walk around the outside to the south wall, you'll see lodged in the stone actual fragments of the heavy equipment used by the Nazis to tear down the Old Town.

In the Old Town

Head a little further north to the heart of the Old Town, the
lively **Old Town Market Square** (Rynek Starego Miasta). The
compact square is one of Poland's finest, an unusually harmonious colourful ensemble of mostly four-level 16th- to
18th-century (style) merchants' houses, each with wonderful
individual Gothic, Baroque and Renaissance architectural features. And it's simply an amazing rebuilding story; it's hard
to believe the square is a replica of what stood here before
the war. In the centre of the Rynek are two water pumps and
a statue of Syrena, the Warsaw mermaid of ancient legend.
The square is popular with visitors, who frequent the roster
of excellent, if relatively expensive, restaurants in the ground
floors and cellars of several of the town houses. The area is
particularly lively in summer, when it's covered with café tables, there are artists and buskers aplenty, and horse-drawn
carriages trundle to and fro for the delight of the tourists.

Old Town Market Square

In the northwest corner of the Rynek is the rambling **Historical Museum of Warsaw** (Muzeum Historyczne Miasta Warszawy; Rynek Starego Miasta 28–42; open Tues and Thur 11am–6pm, Wed and Fri 10.30am–3.30pm, Sat–Sun 10.30am–4.30pm; admission fee). A documentary film, *Warsaw Will Never Forget*, shows the extent of the wartime destruction, and efforts to rebuild the city. The rest of the museum extends across four floors and some 60 rooms of

Syrena, the mermaid of Warsaw, in the city's Market Square

several neighbouring town houses, taking a detailed approach to the city's complicated history. There are city drawings and engravings, a sizeable exhibit on recent archaeological excavations, an interesting mock-up of an 18th-century burgher's house, armaments, documents of the resistance movement, Nazi uniforms and much more. The museum is an unending labyrinth, with most explanations in Polish only, and guards will make you follow its trajectory in a chronological order.

Beyond the Market Square, the cobblestone streets lead to attractive little corners, quiet courtyards and tight passageways. It's a great place to wander, day or night, though you should of course exercise caution after dark. Don't miss the area behind the cathedral, where you'll find a small, pretty square (Kanonia) and a terrace with views across the Vistula. Northwest of the Rynek, on ul. Podwale, is the **Monument to the Little Insurgent**, a bronze statue of a small boy hidden under a giant military helmet and carrying an automatic

The Gothic Barbican

rifle, a symbol of the young children who fought alongside adults in the 1944 Warsaw Uprising against the Nazis. North of the Market Square, ul. Nowowiejska leads to defensive walls, largely rebuilt, and the semicircular Gothic **Barbican** (Barbakan), standing over a moat at what was the northern gate to the city. The area is a popular haunt of street artists and entertainers.

Beyond the Barbican is the **New Town** (Nowe Miasto), where Warsaw expanded after outgrowing the walled Old Town in the 15th century. The two parts were not officially linked until the 18th century. Since it was created as a separate town, the New Town not only has a similar layout to the Old Town, it has its own parish church and town hall. There are several churches in the New Town, including the diminutive Baroque **Church of the Nuns of the Holy Sacrament** (Kościół Sakramentek) on the New Town Market Square (Rynek Nowego Miasta).

Look also for the **Maria Skłodowska-Curie Museum** (Muzeum Marii Skłodowskiej-Curie; ul. Freta 16; open Tues 8.30am–4pm, Wed–Fri 9.30am–4pm, Sat 10am–4pm, Sun 10am–3pm; admission fee), just down the street from the Barbican. Maria Skłodowska (1867–1934), or Marie Curie as she's better known, was born here in Warsaw, though she lived most of her adult life in France. A scientist and physician, she was the first woman to teach at the Sorbonne in Paris. She discovered radium and polonium (named in honour of her native country) and the phenomenon of radioactivity, and won the Nobel Prize in 1903 (for physics) and in 1911 (for chemistry).

When you need a break from sightseeing, keep in mind that the New Town is also known for its restaurants and cafés.

## The Royal Way

The **Royal Way** is the elegant 4-km (2.5-mile) route along which the Polish monarchy travelled south from their official residence, the Royal Castle, to the summer palace, Łazienki. The route is lined with palaces, churches, town houses, museums and monuments along or just off the main streets of ul. Krakowskie Przedmieście, ul. Nowy Świat and al. Ujazdowskie.

Ul. Krakowskie Przedmieście, the first stretch of the route, is one of Warsaw's classic streets. **St Anne's Church** (Kościół Św. Anny; ul. Krakowskie Przedmieście 68) was built in the 15th century, then rebuilt in the Baroque style after Swedes burned it. One of few major churches to avoid devastation in World War II, its observation tower has great views of the Royal Castle and Old Town. To take a detour, walk a couple of blocks west along ul. Senatorska to pl. Teatralny, which is dominated by the **Teatr Wielki – Opera Narodowa** (Great Theatre – National Opera; pl. Teatralny 1), Poland's greatest opera and ballet institution, built in 1833. It was bombed during World War II, with only its façade surviving the blasts.

Back on ul. Krakowskie Przedmieście, as you head south, you'll pass a **statue of Adam Mickiewicz**, Poland's revered Romantic poet. Further south is the white neo-Classical **Radziwiłł Palace**, the residence of the president of Poland. At the front are four stone lions and a statue of Prince Józef Poniatowski, the 19th-century commander-in-chief of the Polish army during Napoleon's Duchy of Warsaw. Across the street is the **Potocki Palace**, now housing the Ministry of Arts and Culture, as well as a gallery of contemporary art. Past the grand Bristol Hotel, built at the turn of the 20th century, is the 18th-century Baroque **Church of the Nuns of the Visitation** (Kościół Wizytek w Warszawie), with a monument to Cardinal Stefan Wyszyński (1901–81), the Primate of Poland from 1948.

West of the Royal Way, in the midst of Ogród Saski gardens, is the **Tomb of the Unknown Soldier**. Housed within the surviving fragments of the 17th-century Saxon Palace, it was placed here in 1925 as the only section of the palace to survive Nazi bombing. The nearby Metropolitan office building was designed by noted British architect Sir Norman Foster.

South of Potocki Palace, **Warsaw University** is denoted by massive, handsome gates atop which perches the traditional Polish eagle. It is the capital's top institution of higher learning, in perpetual rivalry with Kraków's Jagiellonian University. Several of the buildings are former palaces; the

Tomb of the Unknown Soldier

oldest dates from 1634. The **Church of the Holy Cross** (Kościół Św. Krzyża; ul. Krakowskie Przedmieście 3), across the street from the university, is a mausoleum of sorts for famous Poles, among them the composer Frédéric Chopin. In fact, in

**Tram tours**

Using one of the tram routes in Warsaw (there are around 30 of them in total) is an excellent way to get around. Tram stops and routes are marked in red on most city maps.

accordance with his will, only his heart is here, in an urn; the rest of his remains lie in France.

The statue at a fork in the road is one of Poland's other most famous sons, the great astronomer **Nicolaus Copernicus** (Mikołaj Kopernik). With his theory of a heliocentric universe, Copernicus, as Poles commonly say, 'stopped the sun and moved the earth'. Just beyond this, the boulevard becomes **ul. Nowy Świat**, one of Warsaw's most fashionable, and is lined with chic boutiques and cafés.

Set back from ul. Nowy Świat is Ostrogski Palace, site of the **Frédéric Chopin Museum** (Muzeum Fryderyka Chopina; ul. Okólnik 1; open Tues–Sun 10am–6pm; admission fee; <www.tifc.chopin.pl>). This lovely palace is full of artefacts and memorabilia from the life of this outstanding classical composer. Nearby are several others, the Zamoyski Palace (on ul. Foksal), Przezdziecki Palace and Branicki Palace (ul. Smolna).

The **National Museum** (Muzeum Narodowe; al. Jerozolimskie 3; open Tues–Thur 10am–6pm, Fri 10am–8pm, Sat–Sun 10am–5pm; admission fee; <www.mnw.art.pl>) holds a huge collection of art – from Roman and Egyptian archaeology and medieval art to antique furniture and large galleries of Polish and European painting. Ujazdowskie Avenue is lined with embassies in elegant palaces, and nearby are the Sejm (Polish Parliament) and two attractive parks, Ujazdowskie and Łazienkowski, the latter especially esteemed by Varsovians.

**Memorial at the cemetery**

## Jewish Warsaw

Thousands of Jews arrived in Warsaw in the second half of the 14th century, though they were expelled by royal decree not long after. They were finally allowed to settle in the city again in 1768, and by the start of World War II, approximately 350,000, or 30 percent, of Warsaw's citizens were Jews. It was at that time the largest Jewish community in pre-war Europe. The residential Jewish Quarter, around the Mirów and Muranów districts (between the Palace of Culture and Science and the Jewish Cemetery in the northwest corner of the city), was transformed into a ghetto by the Nazis. After the Warsaw Ghetto Uprising in 1943, German troops moved in and liquidated the ghetto.

Today only about 2,000 Jews live in Warsaw. The most obvious reminders of the former Jewish presence are the dilapidated buildings on **ul. Próżna**. A Jewish foundation has been entrusted with the restoration of these buildings, but for the time being they are poignant reminders of devastation. The **Nożyk Synagogue** (Synagoga Nożyków; ul. Twarda 6), still in use, is the only surviving Jewish house of prayer in the city. Another haunting symbol of Jewish martyrdom is the fragment of the **Ghetto Wall** (ul. Sienna 55), constructed in 1940.

Farther north, the **Jewish Cemetery** (Cmentarz Żydowski), which abuts the Powązkowski Cemetery *(see opposite)* and was founded in 1780, gives the overpowering impression of neglect: many of the 150,000 gravestones are toppled over and branches have grown over the tops of them. It seems a shame, but you quickly realise that the Jewish population of Warsaw (and indeed, Poland) was decimated during the war, and most of the people buried here in all probability simply have no family to care for the gravesites. A monument on ul. Stawki marks the spot where 300,000 Jews were transported by train from the ghetto to the Treblinka concentration camp.

On ul. Zamenhofa, the **Monument to the Heroes of the Ghetto** is a tribute to the poorly armed but valiant Jews who rose up against their Nazi oppressors in 1943. The monument, in the spot where the month-long fighting was heaviest, is a bas-relief that incorporates stone that had been ordered by the Third Reich to commemorate its planned victory.

Monument to the Heroes of the Ghetto

## West of the Old Town

The **Powązkowski Cemetery** (Cmentarz Powązkowski; ul. Powàzkowska 14) is Warsaw's oldest, largest and most spectacular necropolis, with a host of Warsaw's and Poland's most distinguished citizens, from presidents to poets, in their final resting places. The cemetery is jam-packed with gravestones and mausoleums of all shapes and sizes, many obvious testaments to the wealth and prestige of those they shelter. Some are grand, some restrained, some crowned by beautifully expressive sculpture, but all are covered by a fuzzy light green moss.

Warsaw's **New City Centre**, near the central train station (Warszawa Centralna), roughly equidistant between the Old Town and Łazienki Park, is a busy commercial area, teeming with banks, hotels and shops, and thick with traffic. It's perhaps most notable for the presence of a building that has become a symbol of the city, despite being abhorred by almost all Varsovians. The **Palace of Culture and Science** (Pałac Kultury i Nauki; pl. Defilad 1), a 1955 Stalinist edifice that was ostensibly a gift of the Russian government to the Polish people, is Warsaw's tallest building, at 231m (758ft). Inside are many shops and galleries, and an observation deck on the 30th floor affords views of the entire city and surrounding Mazovian plains – when not obscured by smog. Since the collapse of Communism, there has been much debate about what to do with this unpopular building.

## Łazienki Palace

The magnificent **Łazienki Palace and Garden Complex** (Łazienki Królewskie; ul. Agrykoli 1; open Tues–Sun 9am–4pm; admission fee) is the former summer residence of King Stanisław August Poniatowski, Poland's final monarch. At the time of its completion in 1793, the so-called Palace on the Water was far removed from the capital. Today, though, the 74-hectare (183-acre) park, opened to the public in 1818, lies right on the fringes of

### Chopin in summer

If you are visiting Warsaw in summer, visit the Monument to Frédéric Chopin (*see opposite*) on a Sunday afternoon, when concerts are held. The combination of the statue, lake and surrounding park create an ideal setting for Chopin's romantic music.

downtown Warsaw. The original 17th-century bathing pavilion was reshaped by the Italian architect Dominic Merlini into a magnificent Classical palace. Other buildings, including a theatre and the White House (Biały Dom) villa, along with several pavilions, orangeries, paths and canals, were added, transforming the complex into a handsome mixture of French classical and Baroque architecture and English-style gardens. The peaceful park is a favourite strolling ground for many inhabitants.

In the grounds of Łazienki Park

In the main building, the Palace on the Island, the neo-Classical Ballroom, Salamon Room and Art Gallery, which once displayed some 2,500 works of art (the most valuable of which were stolen or destroyed, though it still contains pieces from the collection of Stanisław August), are especially notable, as is the Dining Room, where the king held his celebrated 'Thursday dinners' with cultural and political figures. The Bacchus Room is decorated with original Delft tiles.

At the opposite end of the park, overlooking the Vistula Escarpment, is a recreation of the 1926 Secessionist **Monument to Frédéric Chopin**, depicting the composer under a willow tree, which is made to look like his piano-playing hand. The monument – which was reportedly the first destroyed by the Nazis – forms a popular outdoor venue for summer concerts.

## Wilanów

About 6km (4 miles) south of Łazienki is **Wilanów Palace** (Pałac w Wilanowie; ul. Potockiego 10–16, Wilanów; open Sun–Mon and Wed–Fri 9am–4pm, Sat 10am–4pm; admission fee; <www.wilanow-palac.art.pl>), another royal summer residence, dating from 1679. Originally a grand old manor house, this Baroque gem was modelled on Versailles and surrounded by magnificent gardens. Villa Nuova (which became 'Wilanów' in Polish) was the favourite spot of King John III Sobieski, who saved Vienna from the Turks in 1683. After his death, Wilanów was passed among a long line of Polish aristocratic occupants, who altered and extended it. Wilanów was the last private residence nationalised by the new Communist government after World War II. The Czartoryski family, the noble family of art collectors that bequeathed their palace-museum to the city of Kraków, was one of the owners.

Sundial on the exterior of Wilanów Palace

Even though many of the most valuable works of art were either stolen or destroyed, the palace, which didn't suffer great damage during World War II, still contains one of the largest collections of Polish portraits from the 16th to 19th centuries. The ground floor of the palace is the most opulent; the Great Crimson Room is a dining hall dis-

In the gardens of Wilanów

guised as a painting gallery. After your tour, be sure to walk around the Italian gardens, noticing the palace's fine Baroque exterior decoration, the Anglo-Chinese park, and the pond and Roman bridge. Near the entrance to the palace grounds, somewhat incongruously, sits the **Poster Museum** (Muzeum Plakatu; ul. Potockiego 10–16, Wilanów; open Tues–Sun 10am–4pm, Mon noon–4pm; admission fee), dedicated to the high quality of international poster art, a medium still highly respected today.

## ŁÓDŹ

With approximately 770,000 inhabitants, **Łódź** (pronounced 'woodge'), about 100km (60 miles) southwest of Warsaw, is the second-largest city in Poland, with light industry and about half of Polish textile production located within its boundaries. Łódź was granted a town charter as long ago as 1423, but in 1820 still only had 800 inhabitants. Things began to change in 1823 with the building of the New Town (Nowe Miasto), the first textile workers' estate. The removal of the customs barriers between Poland and Russia led to an enormous increase in the export of textiles to Russia, and in the late 19th century Łódź became one of the world's most important textile centres.

During World War II, the Germans opened two large transit camps in Łódź for Polish prisoners-of-war, as well as a camp for Russian airmen, a camp for 5,000 gypsies from Germany, Austria and the Balkans, and also a camp for 4,000 Polish children. Approximately 260,000 Jews were murdered in nearby Chełmno and Nerem, and the people of Łódź itself were also affected; of its 600,000 inhabitants only half survived the war.

After the war new housing and industrial estates grew up around the original districts of the town. In addition to the traditional textile industry, electrical engineering and chemical industries also came to Łódź. The first institutions of further education were founded, the most famous being the State College of Cinematic Art, Drama and Television. The University of Łódź has a Department of Polish language for foreigners.

## Main Sights

Łódź's star attraction is ul. Piotrkowska, its huge, 5-km (3-mile) pedestrian street cutting the city neatly in two. Lined by

### Łódź Film School

In his autobiography, Roman Polański writes: 'It was through a mere whim of history that Łódź became the film capital of Poland…after the war the capital, Warsaw, lay in ruins and…the government chose the nearest suitable town when looking for a place to establish a centre of cinematography.' Two years after World War II the Kraków film course transferred to Łódź and from then on it was here that filmmakers received their training. Polański, whose films include *Rosemary's Baby* and *Chinatown*, is probably the school's most celebrated director, but other alumni include director Andrzej Wajda (*The Promised Land, The Iron Man* and *Danton*) and Krzysztof Kieslowski (*The Double Life of Véronique, Three Colours: Blue, White, Red*).

some of the city's finest buildings, of which many house hotels, restaurants and bars, the summer sees the street come alive with scores of lively terraces scattered all the way down. The **Textile Museum** (Muzeum Włókiennictwa; ul. Piotrkowska 282; open Tues–Wed and Fri 9am–5pm, Thur 11am–7pm, Sat–Sun 11am–4pm; admission fee; <www. muzeumwlokiennictwa.pl>) is located here in the White Factory. It portrays the development of technology in the textile industry, and houses a fine collection of 16th-century to modern textiles from all over the world.

There are two further museums of note in the city. The **Museum of Art** (Muzeum Sztuki; ul. Wiąckowskiego 36;

Poznański Palace

open Tues 10am–5pm, Wed and Fri 11am–5pm, Thur noon–7pm, Sat–Sun 10am–4pm; admission fee; <www. muzeumsztuki.lodz.pl>), in the palace once owned by the Poznański family, exhibits Polish and international art from the 19th century onwards. The **History of Łódź Museum** (Muzeum Historii Miasta Łodzi; ul. Ogrodowa 15; open Sat–Mon 10am–2pm, Tues and Thur 10am–4pm, Wed 2–6pm; admission fee; <www.poznanskipalace. muzeum-lodz.pl>), accommodated in another of the Poznańskis' palaces, documents the town's past, showing how it looked prior to

World War II's devastation. Also on display is the memorabilia of Artur Rubinstein, the famous pianist and composer, who was born here. The excellent Philharmonic Hall of Łódź has been named after him.

Before the war over 30 percent of the inhabitants of Łódź were Jewish. The Jewish community, both synagogues and the old Jewish cemetery were destroyed during the war. Only the new Jewish Cemetery survived, with around 120,000 gravestones and the **Izrael Poznański Mausoleum** erected between 1893 and 1939. Today it is allegedly the largest Jewish cemetery in Europe and one of the largest in the world.

# GDAŃSK

The northern city of **Gdańsk** catapulted to the world's attention as the focus of struggles between Polish workers and the

Rooftops in the Old Town (Long Street), Gdańsk

Communist regime in the early 1980s. Images of the Gdańsk shipyards were beamed into living rooms around the world. The Solidarność, or Solidarity, workers' union not only helped set in motion a movement that would eventually topple governments throughout the Soviet Union, its leader, Lech Wałęsa – a shipyard electrician – became the first democratically elected president of post-Communist Poland in 1990.

Though Gdańsk's recent history has grabbed headlines, this city on the Baltic Sea has long been an important, and contentious, place. In 1308, the Teutonic Knights stormed the city, called Danzig by the Germans, and made it their medieval stronghold on the Baltic. It later became a prosperous port and trade centre as part of the Hanseatic League in the 14th century. For two centuries, the city essentially operated as an independent city-state. By the 16th century, Gdańsk was the largest city in Poland and the country's dominant international trade centre. During the Second Partition of Poland at the end of the 18th century, Prussia annexed the city; Napoleon laid siege to it in 1807 and declared it the Free City of Danzig; and the Congress of Vienna in 1815 returned it to Prussia.

Hitler began his acquisitive rampage here, and the assault on the Westerplatte peninsula on 1 September 1939 began World War II. The Old City, a spectacular creation of Gothic, Baroque and Renaissance architecture with a distinct Flemish aesthetic, was obliterated during the war. The city was meticulously rebuilt, and today it is one of the most spectacular of all of Poland's old cities; its Royal Way is breathtaking, even though most of it was reconstructed in the 1950s. Amazingly, Gdańsk looks and feels like a 16th-century city.

Gdańsk is in fact the largest member of a Tri-city (Trójmiasto) region on the Baltic Sea. Gdańsk, Sopot and Gdynia form a 20km (12-mile) conurbation along the bay. While the three cities have retained their own distinct identities, Gdańsk is by far the most important and historic.

## The Main Town

Gdańsk is unusual among Polish cities. It has three distinct historic areas, but the Old Town is not in fact the birthplace of the city, and it doesn't possess the finest architectural ensemble. That distinction falls to the **Main Town** (Główne Miasto), often confused with the Old Town.

Golden Gate

### The Royal Way

Gdańsk, despite its tortuous history of shifting allegiances, was loyal to the Polish crown for three centuries. When the king would travel from the capital, Warsaw, to the largest port (and provider of tax income), he would enter Gdańsk through a series of formal gates and down the extraordinary main thoroughfare. Kraków and Warsaw also have Royal Ways, but neither is as stunning as the one in Gdańsk. It is one of the undisputed highlights of Poland.

The king first passed through the brick **Upland Gate** (Brama Wyżynna), dating from the 16th century, where he was given the keys to the city. Beyond the Upland Gate is the **Golden Gate** (Złota Brama), a more ornamental structure formed by an arch topped by allegorical figures. The gate was added in 1644 but only recently fully restored to its original gilded splendour. Royal processions would then proceed onto **Long Street** (ul. Długa), a pedestrian-only promenade lined with magnificent, brilliantly coloured three- and four-storey houses with fine Baroque portals, Gothic moldings, Renaissance façades, coats of arms and whimsical decorations. Most were rebuilt after World War

II, which left the promenade in total ruins. A few original details did survive. Pause to admire house numbers 28, 29, 35 and 71. Of particular interest is **Uphagen's House** (Dom Uphagena; ul. Długa 12; open Wed–Sat 10am–4pm, Sun 11am–4pm, Tues 10am–3pm; admission fee), a museum occupying a splendid 18th-century merchant's house, with displays of textiles and rich period furnishings.

At the end of ul. Długa is the 14th-century **Main Town Hall** (Ratusz Głównego Miasta; ul. Długa 46–7; open Wed–Sat 10am–4pm, Sun 11am–4pm, Tues 10am–3pm; admission fee), crowned by a tall spire and life-size golden statue of King Sigismund August. The seat of the municipal government, it is one of the focal points of the Royal Way. The opulent interior, rich with oil paintings and frescoes, houses the **Gdańsk History Museum** (Muzeum Historyczne Miasta Gdańska; for information on the city's museums see <www.mhmg.gda.pl>), where you'll find a fine collection of photographs of the city before and after World War II. The fabulous Red Room, which once held Council debates, is all original; its decorative elements were dismantled and hidden during the war. Don't miss the views of the city from the top of the tower.

Just in front of the Town

Neptune Fountain, symbol of the city of Gdańsk

Golden House

Hall is the **Neptune Fountain** (Fontanna Neptuna), a Flemish artist's beautiful bronze sculpture of the god of the sea, created in 1549 and converted into a fountain nearly a century later. It is said to be the oldest secular monument in Poland. Such was the locals' attachment to the fountain that they dismantled it piece-by-piece and hid it during World War II, finally returning it to its original place in 1954. Neptune stands at the head of the second major section of the Royal promenade, **Long Market** (Długi Targ). Several of the most attractive houses in Gdańsk face the long market, which is more a boulevard than a square. Particularly impressive is the mansion **Artus Court** (Dwór Artusa; Długi Targ 43–4; open Wed–Sat 10am–4pm, Sun 11am–4pm, Tues 10am–3pm; admission fee), a former meeting place for Gdańsk merchants, named after the court of King Arthur. Inside the massive hall, now a museum, is an immense mid-16th-century tiled stove, with a stunning assembly of more than 500 decorative tiles.

On the same side of the street is the **Golden House** (Złota Kamienica; Długi Targ 41–2), perhaps the most beautiful in the Old Town. The four-storey stucture dates from the 17th century. The magnificent façade, thoroughly restored in 2001, is decorated with rich allegorical friezes, busts of historical figures, and at the top, four statues of gesticulating characters from classical mythology. Home to the Cunard shipping line between the wars, the building is now the Maritime Institute.

At the far end of Long Market is the **Green Gate** (Zielona Brama), a massive and bold, four-arched structure. More a building than a gate, it was intended to be a palace for visiting kings, though the exceedingly cold interior scared them away and no Polish monarch ever slept at the Green Gate.

*Waterfront*

Pass through the Green Gate and you'll discover the waterfront of the Motlawa River. The **Great Crane** (Żuraw), the largest in medieval Europe, is a giant gate built in 1444 to lift massive cargo onto ships and install ship masts. The crane now forms part of the sprawling **Central Maritime Museum** (Centralne Muzeum Morskie; ul. Ołowianka 9–13; open Tues–Sun 10am–3pm; admission fee; <www.cmm. pl>), which expands across both sides of the river. It has a collection of antique shipping vessels and boats and, in three restored old granaries across the river, exhibits documenting Polish seafaring history, including Swedish canons from the 17th-century Deluge. A boat shuttles visitors back and forth across the Motlawa river, and you can also step aboard the *Sołdek*, Gdańsk's first cargo ship built after World War II.

Gdańsk waterfront

Return to the interior of the city through **St Mary's Gate** (Brama Św. Marii), a medieval defensive gate, which leads to the quiet but exceedingly evocative cobblestoned street, **ul. Mariacka**. It is one of the prettiest in Poland, with unique terraces and carved gargoyle drainpipes decorating every house. Like others in Gdańsk, this street was reconstructed after the war, but it lost none of its charm. Many of the houses are now jewellery shops specialising in amber, the local semi-precious stone (it's actually fossilised tree resin).

The street terminates in the red-brick Gothic **St Mary's Church** (Kościół Mariacki; ul. Podkramarska 5). The massive structure, begun in the 14th century but not finished until 150 years later, is one of the world's largest churches, said to be capable of holding up to 25,000 worshippers. Indeed, it is far more impressive for its sheer size than its exterior beauty. The interior is vast but somewhat plain, a result of war damage. Impressive frescoes were whitewashed. The Gothic vault interior retains 31 chapels, three dozen large windows and one amazing **astronomical clock**. The 15th-century clock features zodiac signs, phases of the moon, time and date, and a cast of characters that peep out to celebrate the tolling of the hour. Adam and Eve ring the bell, while the 12 apostles emerge from the right side. The clock comes with a cruel twist: it is said that its maker's eyes were put out, by order of the mayor, so that he might

Royal Chapel

never again build a clock to compete with this one.

In the shadow of the St Mary's behemoth is the **Royal Chapel**, a small 17th-century Baroque Catholic church with a richly ornamented exterior. It is believed to be the work of Tylman of Gameron, a Dutch architect. The dome-topped church was built for the city's then Catholic minority to comply with the will of the Primate of Poland. At the time, Gdańsk was a mainly Protestant city.

Just west of St Mary's (Targ Węglowy 6) is the landmark **Great Armoury**. Built in 1609 at the edge of the city's medieval walls, it is a huge Renaissance building with a spectacular façade, of marked Flemish influence. A great deal of work went into designing a building that would do little more than store armaments. Restored following damage caused during World War II, it now has another prosaic inhabitant – a shopping mall. The other side, which faces Targ Węglowy, is less ornate.

Wedged into a side street at the northern edge of the Main Town is **St Nicholas' Church** (Kościół Św. Mikołaja; ul. Świętojańska 72). Unlike much of the city, the Dominican church escaped major war damage. The light interior has a quite stunning collection of 10 black-and-gold Baroque altarpieces affixed to columns on either side of a central nave. It also features a gilded, tiered high altar and impressive Baroque pipe organ. A children's choir sings on Sunday mornings.

## Goldwasser

Gdańsk is famous as the birthplace of *Goldwasser* (gold water), which is vodka with added 23-carat gold leaf – once thought to have medicinal benefits. Whether the gold contributed to its flavour is a matter of opinion, but with this rich, sweet vodka, flavoured with a blend of herbs and spices, there is plenty to savour. Goldwasser was also renowned as the most expensive vodka, giving it added cachet.

## Old Town

The **Old Town** (Stare Miasto) developed in tandem with the Main Town, though it was never as wealthy and after the war was not as lovingly or thoroughly rebuilt. Consequently, it has fewer sights of interest, but enough for a half-day's exploration.

Of principal interest is the **Great Mill** (Wielki Młyn; ul. Wielkie Młyny 16), a terrific structure with a sloping tiled roof. Built by the Teutonic Knights in 1350, the mill was the largest in medieval Europe, and it continued to function until the end of World War II. Today, however, it houses an indoor shopping mall with all manner of clothing stores. Past

Monument of the Fallen Shipyard Workers

the small pond behind the mill and across the street is Gdańsk's **Old Town Hall** (Ratusz Starego Miasta; ul. Korzenna 33–5; open Mon–Fri 9am–5pm), a 16th-century building that was labelled the pearl of the Dutch Renaissance. Designed by Antoon van Opberghen, who also designed the Great Armoury, this is where the town council met. It now contains a café and exhibition centre, but of greatest interest is the rich interior. Walk in and take a look upstairs, where you'll find the Great Hall.

Directly across the street from the Great Mill is **St Catherine's Church** (Kościół Św. Katarzyny; ul. Profesorska 3), the former parish church and the oldest church in Gdańsk, begun in 1220. The Gothic-vaulted interior is most appreciated for the enormous mural, on the left aisle beneath the organ loft, depicting Christ's entry into Jerusalem. The church tower holds a 37-bell carillon that chimes on the hour. The church was damaged by fire in 2006, and access is currently limited to the area under the main tower. Restoration work is expected to carry on well into 2008.

Directly behind, or east of, St Catherine's is **St Bridget's Church** (Kościół Św. Brygidy; ul. Profesorska 17), which dates from the 15th century, but more recently became a refuge for the Solidarity movement from the Communist government. Inside are several permanent displays related to the human rights struggles of the Polish workers' union. In fact, Lech Wałęsa attended Mass here before he became the spokesman for Solidarność. The politicised nature of the church is evident on the right aisle in a series of crosses from the 1980s strikes, the gravestone of murdered priest (and Solidarność sympathizer) Jerzy Popiełuszko, and a bas-relief history of the workers' union.

A 10-minute walk north takes you to the old Gdańsk shipyards, where the Solidarity union protests took root. Today the shipyard is quiet, though there's a huge **Monument of the Fallen Shipyard Workers** (Pomnik Poległych Stoczniowców; pl. Solidarności), an evocative sculpture of crosses and anchors commemorating the 44 who were killed in the 1970 street riots against the Communists. A museum called **Roads to Freedom** (Drogi do Wolności; ul. Wały Piastowskie 24; open Tues–Sun 10am–4pm; admission fee; <www.fcs.org.pl>), detailing the history of Solidarity, has recently moved from its original historic dockyard building to a less meaningful space. Fortunately, the once excellent exhibition is even better than before.

## Old Suburb

South of the Main Town is the third of Gdańsk's historic districts, where the city expanded in the 15th century, now called the **Old Suburb** (Stare Przedmieście). Rebuilt after World War II devastation, there are a couple of essential sights worth checking out. The neighbourhood lies across the major road ul. Podwale Przedmiejskie.

The **National Museum** (Muzeum Narodowe; ul. Toruńska 1; open Tues–Fri 9am–4pm, Sat–Sun 10am–4pm; admission fee; <www.muzeum.narodowe.gda.pl>) is one of Poland's most important repositories of medieval art, tapestries, embroidery, gold and silverware, all housed in a vaulted former Franciscan monastery and hospital. Its most famous work is *The Last Judgement*, a triptych by the 15th-century Dutch painter Hans Memling. The Flemish and Dutch collection also contain works by Van Dyck and Breughel the Younger.

Abutting the museum is the **Church of the Holy Trinity** (Kościół Świętej Trójcy; ul. Św. Trójcy 4), Gdańsk's second-largest church. Built in the 15th century, the well-preserved Gothic structure has a spacious white interior. Of particular interest is the high altar, comprising varied panels in a triptych.

## EXCURSIONS FROM GDAŃSK

**Sopot**, a former fishing village just 12km (7 miles) north of Gdańsk, is one of Poland's most fashionable seaside resorts. It began as a spa town in the 18th century; little damaged by World War II, Sopot has a relaxed, elegant feel, complemented by the early 20th-century Secessionist buildings. The town attracts huge crowds of northern Europeans and Poles in summer months, drawn to the cafés, restaurants and nightclubs along the main pedestrian thoroughfare, ul. Bohaterów Monte Cassino, and its sandy beaches and waters in the Gdańsk Bay (once badly polluted – be aware that the beaches may be closed at any time depending on pollution levels). Sopot also has a 10-km (6-mile) path that runs through the park along the Baltic Sea, ideal for walking, running or cycling. Also popular are the promenade along the 1920s **pier** (Molo Południowe), Poland's longest, and the open-air **Forest Opera House** (Opera Leśna), an amphitheatre in the woods.

The next town north along the bay (some 21km/13 miles from Gdańsk), **Gdynia**, is also a former fishing village, although in the 20th century it was transformed into a large and wealthy industrial port city with boutiques, bars, restaurants and museums that draw visitors from across Poland. The majority of sights, clustered around the pier, are related to the sea and sea-farers. Visit the ship museums (including the *Błyskawica*, a World War II destroyer, and *Dar Pomorza*, a 1909 three-masted frigate), go to the **Oceanographic Museum and Aquarium** (Akwarium Gdyńskie; al. Jana Pawła II 1; open Tues–Sun 10am–5pm; admission fee) or visit the **Naval Museum** (Muzeum Morskie; ul. Zawiszy Czarnego 1a; open Tues–Sun 10am–4pm; admission fee), a museum of Polish warfare currently only partially open to the public.

Hel beach

Both Sopot and Gdynia are easily reached by train (leaving every 10 minutes during the day and less frequently late at night) from the Gdańsk Główny train station. It takes about 20 minutes to Sopot, and 30 minutes to Gdynia.

To escape the crowds, head to the tranquil **Hel Peninsula**, which stretches like a slim finger 35km (20 miles) across

Malbork Castle

the bay. The string of fishing villages and sandy beaches is gaining in popularity as an easy day trip from Gdańsk, Sopot or Gdynia. Trains to Hel leave from Gdynia, and take 2 hours. For tourist information, see <www.jastarnia.pl>.

Alternatively, go inland to the unspoilt **Kashubia** (Kaszuby) region, a hilly land of folk art, an upside-down house and an ethnically distinct people with their own language and customs.

## Malbork Castle

Poland's largest, most famous castle is **Malbork** (Zamek w Malborku; ul. Starościńska 1; open Tues–Sun 9am–7pm; admission fee; <www.zamek.malbork.pl>), about 60km (37 miles) south of Gdańsk. The 14th-century medieval fortress, built by the Order of the Teutonic Knights on the banks of the River Nogat, gives every impression of being impregnable. It is a monumental red brick complex, with turrets, drawbridges and the most solid of walls dominating the flat plains around it.

In 1280, the Teutonic Knights built a fortified monastery, and in 1308, the Grand Master came to live in Malbork, elevating the status of the settlement to headquarters of the entire Order. The interior of the castle is astounding, a labyrinth of seemingly unending rooms and chapels. Highlights include the perfectly harmonious vaulting in the refectory, the stunning Gothic portal known as the Golden Gate, the massive Knight's Hall and the museum collection of amber. Even after the defeat and retreat of the Teutonic Knights, the castle never fell into ruin. It became a residence of the Polish monarchs.

Inclusive visits are by guided tour only, though some parts of the castle complex can be visited on one's own. Getting to Malbork is straightforward. The train journey from Gdańsk Główny train station takes 40 minutes by express train or an hour by regular train. From Malbork town, the castle is an easy 10-minute walk. This impressive landmark is well worth the time.

During summer months, Malbork Castle stages hour-long evening sound-and-light shows in the main courtyard.

# TORUŃ

In the lower Vistula Valley, 182km (113 miles) south of Gdańsk, lies the handsome, historic city of **Toruń**. Founded by the Teutonic Knights in 1233, the medieval walled town sits on the right bank of Poland's greatest river; its positioning allowed it to rise to prominence in the 14th and 15th centuries as a Hanseatic port city. It's probably best known, however, as the birthplace of Mikołaj Kopernik – or, as most people know him, Nicolaus Copernicus, the great 16th-century astronomer.

Toruń's city council outlawed wooden buildings in the 14th century, requiring all the city's important edifices to be made of brick and stone. At the time, the city won accolades as 'beautiful red Toruń'. With a unique collection of Gothic architecture, including a ruined castle, fine churches, fortifications, a leaning tower and the home of Copernicus, Toruń is distinguished as a UNESCO World Heritage Site. Today, the historic centre is a living museum of architecture, with a growing number of cafés, restaurants and shops. It is easily covered on foot, with a day's walking tour taking in all the sights, though you obviously need longer to visit museums.

## Old Town

The core of the city's **Old Town** (Stare Miasto) is its **Old Town Square** (Rynek Staromiejski). In its middle stands the dignified **Town Hall** (Ratusz), a solid Gothic brick construction raised in the 14th century, with Dutch Renaissance turrets and gables (the clock tower, formerly an independent structure, was built in 1247). Suitable for a town known for a mathematician-astronomer, the Town Hall has 12 halls representing the months of the year, 52 small rooms representing the

Toruń's Old Town

number of weeks, and 365 windows for each day of the year. The former municipal seat of government has been almost wholly taken over by the **Regional Museum** (Muzeum Okręgowe; Rynek Staromiejski 1; open Tues–Sun 10am–4pm; admission fee; for information on the city's museums see <www.muzeum.torun.pl>), which displays a fine collection of Gothic art, stained glass and Polish painting amid Gothic interiors with vaulted ceilings. The top of the clock tower affords a sweeping view of Toruń's red-tile roofs and the river.

> ### Toruń gingerbread
>
> Toruń is known for its traditional gingerbread, and its bakers can be pretty creative with the medieval recipe. Look for gingerbread figures of Copernicus, among other fancy creations.

In the southeast corner of the square, in front of the Town Hall, is a statue commemorating Toruń's most famous citizen, **Nicolaus Copernicus**. Across the street is a large, extravagant 19th-century building known as **Arthur's Court** (Dwór Artusa; Rynek Staromiejski 6), formerly a meeting place for town merchants and today the site of a cultural centre. Facing the square on its east side is a pretty yellow four-storey building with an ornate Baroque façade and gabled roof. Called the **House Under the Star** (Pod Gwiazda; Rynek Staromiejski 35; open Tues–Sun 10am–4pm; admission fee), it's a museum displaying art from the Far East. It's also worth seeing its lush interior, which features painted ceilings and the fabulous 17th-century carved-wood spiral staircase that rises three floors.

On the opposite side of the Rynek is the uninspiring 18th-century **Church of the Holy Spirit** (Kościół pw. Ducha Świętego). Between it and the Town Hall is a fountain featuring a slew of frogs and a young boy playing the violin. It represents a legend of a frightening moment when Toruń was invaded by frogs and the boy charmed them back to the woods with his

Copernicus monument

violin. Just off the northwest corner of the square is the imposing **St Mary's Church** (Kościół Mariacki; ul. Panny Marii), a Franciscan monastery from the 13th century. The highlight of the interior is a series of interesting and colourful frescoes on the columns supporting the nave.

Around the corner to the north is Toruń's **Planetarium** (Planetarium im. Władysława Dziewulskiego; ul. Franciszkańska 15–21; admission fee; <www.planetarium.torun.pl>, see website for show times). Installed in a 19th-century gasworks, whose round shape was perfect for its needs, this is the most modern planetarium in Poland. There are afternoon shows daily, though the soundtrack is in Polish. Across the street is Toruń's respected Mikołaj Kopernik University, also a feast of Gothic brick; its **Collegium Maius** (ul. Fosa Staromiejska 3) dates from the end of the 16th century.

Toruń's other major sights are south of the Rynek. The **Copernicus Museum** (Muzeum Kopernika; ul. Kopernika 15–17; open Tues–Sun 10am–4pm; admission fee), inhabits the handsome burgher's house where the astronomer was born in 1473. The museum has a first edition of his seminal work *De Revolutionibus Orbium Coelestium* along with mostly reproductions of the great scientist's instruments, and it also features a very interesting sound-and-light show of Toruń in the 15th century. Directly south of the museum, along ul. Bankowa, are remnants of the city's fortifications. Although good portions of the walls were destroyed during the 17th-century Swedish Deluge, and other sections were torn down to allow the city to expand, four bastions and three gates survive. Nearby are old granaries, the Monastery Gate and the **Leaning Tower** (Krzywa Wieża; Pod Krzywą Wieżą). This last item is curious indeed; it bends noticeably in towards the street. Its structural flaw is explained away by a legend that states that a Teutonic Knight, a monk sworn to chastity, was caught *in flagrante* with a townswoman and made to build a leaning tower to show the harm of deviance from upright moral standards.

## Copernicus

One of the world's most influential astronomers, Mikołaj Kopernik (Nicolaus Copernicus, 1473–1543) was born in Toruń, the son of a prosperous merchant. The house in which Copernicus was born is now a museum detailing his life and works (see *opposite*) and houses the original edition of *De Revolutionibus Orbium Coelestium*, his revolutionary, initially very controversial, theory that the sun, not the earth, was the centre of the universe.

Copernicus allegedly studied at the Jagiellonian University in Kraków. In 1497 he went to Italy to continue his studies; it was there that he witnessed a lunar eclipse, which first led him to question whether the earth was the centre of the universe. It was not until 1543, however, that his book on the subject was published, in Nuremberg. Copernicus – who only saw a copy as he lay dying of a brain haemmorrhage – dedicated the book to Pope Paul III, but the Roman Catholic Church still considered his theories to be 'subversive', and the work was banned until 1757. Yet it provided a basis for subsequent theories by distinguished astronomers including Galileo. The argument over whether Copernicus was actually Polish or German is expected to continue until the universe he first described is no more.

On the corner of ul. Żeglarska and ul. Św. Jana is Torun's largest church, the 13th-century **Cathedral of Saints John the Baptist and John the Evangelist** (Katedra Św. Janów; ul. Żeglarska 16). The immense brick church took a couple of hundred years to complete. Before going in, note the clock on the southern side; added in the 15th century, it still functions today. The spacious interior has Gothic vaulting and a series of attractive chapels and altars. Some frescoes have been uncovered; the most interesting is the monochrome painting of the devil high at the back of the right aisle. A chapel nearby holds a medieval font in which Copernicus was baptised.

Southwest of the cathedral are the ruins of the **Teutonic Castle**, built by the Order in the 13th century. Toruń citizens destroyed it in 1454 (and herded the Order out of town) and it has lain in ruins since. There is just one surviving tower and a covered passageway you can walk through.

## New Town

In contrast to the Old Town, the buildings in the expansion west were built mostly of wood. They didn't survive, so what remain in the New Town (Nowe Miasto) are mainly brick constructions of the 15th and 16th centuries. The **New Town Square** (Rynek Nowomiejski) is less impressive than its older counterpart, but it's worth a look. The major church in this part of town is **St James's Church** (Kościół Św. Jakuba; Rynek Nowomiejski 6), notable for its flying buttresses – unusual for Poland. Inside are some interesting Gothic wall paintings.

Cathedral mural

Castle ruins, Toruń

Walk west to Plac Teatralny, at the edge of the Old Town, where you'll find Toruń's major theatre, the neo-Baroque **Teatr Horzycy** (Plac Teatralny 1). The park across the intersection holds a very interesting skansen, or outdoor **Ethnographic Museum** (Muzeum Etnograficzne w Toruniu; ul. Wały gen. Sikorskiego 19; open Tues–Fri 9am–4pm, Sat–Sun 10am–4pm; admission fee). Dating from 1959, it displays a collection of 18th- to early-20th-century houses moved here from the surrounding region. Once a year, on a Sunday in September, the skansen becomes a living museum with actors playing the parts of blacksmiths and other rural workers.

## Bydgoszcz

Just 45km (28 miles) northwest of Toruń and easily reached by bus and train is the charming yet overlooked city of **Bydgoszcz**, sitting in Gothic, Renaissance and Art Nouveau splendour on the banks of the Brda River. Highlights include the extraordinary painted interior of **SS Martin and Nicholas' Cathedral**, the quirky and original Pharmacy Museum and the handful of poignant sights connected with Bydgoszcz-born Marian Rejewski (1905–80), the mathematician who first cracked Germany's Enigma code.

# POZNAŃ

Halfway between Berlin and Warsaw, **Poznań** is the principal city of Wielkopolska, a region in western Poland that is one of the country's largest and most historic. Wielkopolska means Great Poland, a title that reflects its role in the development of the Polish nation. Wielkopolska is effectively the birthplace of Poland: in the 10th century, Prince Mieszko succeeded in uniting the Polanie (literally, 'people of the fields') and neighbouring Slavic tribes, founding the Polish state in 966.

> ### Bleat the clock
>
> Crowds gather daily at noon beneath the tower of the Town Hall to see two mechanical billy goats emerge from the parapet in the clock tower. A 16th-century tradition, the metal goats butt horns 12 times to signal the hour.

Until the royals adopted Kraków in 1038, Poznań was in essence the capital of Poland. The city began its development on the island of Ostrów Tumski and the new town centre was begun in the 13th century. In the 18th century, it fell to the Prussians under the Second Partition and became increasingly Germanic, a trait for which it is known today throughout Poland. In modern times, Poznań is best known for a tragic episode: in 1956, a workers' strike was crushed by the Communist government, leaving 76 people dead and nearly 1,000 injured.

Today Poznań is one of the most dynamic and prosperous cities in Poland, with an attractive historic core, a wealth of

Gothic, Renaissance and neo-Classical architecture, and a civic commitment to business development and international trade fairs. Citizens of Poznań are sometimes chided by other Poles for being a bit too industrious and money-minded, but their work ethic is the reason the city is second behind Warsaw in terms of international investment. Poznań draws large numbers of business visitors to its many trade fairs, but the city also enchants leisure-minded visitors, who concentrate on three primary areas: the Stary Rynek, or Old Market Square, the Ostrów Tumski island and the New Town (Nowe Miasto).

## Old Market Square

In Poznań you will find the **Old Market Square** (Stary Rynek), one of the largest and finest in Poland. The fairytale **Town Hall** (Ratusz), a fanciful construction of Italian Renaissance designed by Giovanni Battista di Quadro, replaced

Poznań's Old Market Square

the original, smaller Gothic 14th-century structure, which was destroyed by a devastating fire in 1536. The building, constructed in the 1550s, features a splendid three-storey Renaissance, arcaded loggia and a classical tower, added in 1783, topped by the Polish eagle. The brilliant colours of the frieze above the loggia, depicting the Jagiellonian dynasty kings, have recently been restored to their original splendour, returning the building to its status as one of the most distinctive in Poland. Adding to the sites of interest, just in front of the Town Hall is a copy of a 1535 pillory, with a Rococo **Proserpina Fountain** dating from the 18th century.

The Town Hall holds the **History Museum of Poznań**

Town Hall

(Muzeum Historii Miasta Poznania; Stary Rynek 1; open Tues and Thur–Fri 9am–4pm, Wed 11am–6pm, Sat 10am–4pm, Sun 10am–3pm; admission fee). The Great Hall is a spectacular vaulted room with a Renaissance ceiling, rich with stucco decoration, coats of arms, symbols of the heavens and exotic animals. The museum displays a collection of art, medieval sculpture, distinctive 'coffin portraits' (paintings of the deceased attached to their caskets) and Poznań crafts from the 10th to the mid-20th century. In the Court Chamber, there are frescoes representing the four continents then known – Europe, Asia, Africa and America. Interestingly enough the vaulted Gothic cellars survive from the original town hall.

Adjoining the Town Hall to the south is a row of narrow and colourful fish sellers' houses, built in the 1500s. Lining the four sides of the square are elegant and colourful arcaded burghers' houses and two magnificent palaces. Many remarkable

Café in the Old Market Square

edifices had to be rebuilt in the 1950s, following World War II, to their original Gothic, Baroque and Renaissance designs. Almost all of the Rynek's houses have vaulted medieval cellars, several of which have been converted into atmospheric restaurants. Some of the best preserved include No. 37, today the Maison de la Bretagne, but formerly the oldest pharmacy in Poznań – and Nos 40, 41, 42 and 43. No. 41 is a still a pharmacy, established in 1564, the White Eagle. On the façade of the **Henryk Sienkiewicz Literature Museum** (Muzeum Literackie Henryka Sienkiewicza; Stary Rynek 84; open Mon–Fri 10am–5pm; admission fee), you'll see a statue of the Italian architect, Battista di Quadro, who lived in this house while building the Town Hall.

The 18th-century **Działyński Palace**, at the corner of ul. Frańciszkańska on the west side of the square, is a lovely classical structure painted a light shade of green and decorated with sculptures and reliefs. On top is a pelican, symbolic of Poznań's rebirth after the Partition of Poland. More spectacular than the façade is the Red Room, where 'literary Thursdays' were held in the period between the world wars. The palace at No. 91 belonged to the Mielżyński family.

## Musical interlude

The Museum of Musical Instruments (Muzeum Instrumentów Muzycznych; Stary Rynek 45–7; open Tues–Sat 11am–5pm, Sun 11am–3pm; admission fee) is the only one of its kind in Poland. Inside you'll find early phonographs, church and Polish-army drums, a Celtic horn, 17th-century Polish violins from Groblicz, and a pianoforte once played by Chopin, as well as odd Polish folk instruments and exotic drums from around the world.

The middle of the square is also occupied by a large, incongruous and unattractive 1950s- and 1960s-era pavilion, which was constructed after the war on the sites of the old cloth hall and arsenal, and houses the **Galeria Miejska Arsenał** contemporary art gallery (Stary Rynek 3; open Tues–Sat 11am–6pm, Sun 11am–3pm; admission fee). The building mars the otherwise exquisite harmony of the square, and while there have been discussions in the municipal government about tearing it down or adding façades more consistent with the Renaissance appearance of the square, any such action is unlikely.

In a passageway between the pavilion and Town Hall is the cute **Monument of a Bamberg Woman** in folkloric dress on the way to a well, with large jugs in both hands. The statue pays tribute to 18th-century immigrants to Poznań from Bamberg, Germany. Also of note is the **June 1956 Poznań Uprising Museum** (Muzeum Powstania Poznańskiego – Czerwiec 1956; ul. Św. Marcina 80–2; open Tues–Fri and Sun 10am–6pm, Sat 10am–4pm; admission fee), a small but poignant museum portraying the days of unrest in the city during that year.

One of Poznań's most stately residences is the **Górka Palace**, built in the mid-16th century and occupying an entire block on the corner of Wodna and Świętosławska streets (southeast corner of the Stary Rynek). Note the Renaissance portals; in the interior is a beautiful arcaded courtyard. The palace passed from the Górkas, one of Poznań's most powerful families, to Benedictine nuns during the Reformation; today it is the site of the **Archaeological Museum** (Muzeum Archeologiczne; ul. Wodna 27; open Tues–Fri 10am–4pm, Sat 10am–6pm, Sun 10am–3pm; admission fee), displaying a collection of artefacts dating to the prehistory and foundations of Wielkopolska as well as ancient Egypt. New excavations and restoration are ongoing at the site.

During the summer, the Stary Rynek is full of lively outdoor cafés, and concerts and performances are frequently staged here. At night the square is beautifully illuminated and a wonderful place to take a stroll.

## Around Old Market Square

A block south of Górka Palace is Poznań's stunning salmon-coloured **Parish Church of St Stanislaus** (Kościół Św.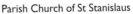

Parish Church of St Stanislaus

Raczyński Library

Stanisława; ul. Gołębia 1). A Jesuit church until 1701, it is one of the most important Roman Baroque churches in Poland. Though not greatly damaged by the war, the Baroque interior, with beautiful stucco work and murals, is in the process of being meticulously restored. Like Michelangelo's Sistine Chapel, its refurbished colours are so bright that the restoration has attracted criticism. Note the curious flat cupola that is in fact an optical illusion, giving the impression of being a dome. The church organ is an excellent 19th-century example of the work of Friedrich Ladegast.

Adjoining the Parish Church, the handsome orange-pink collection of buildings, formerly the Jesuit College, now house Poznań's municipal government.

West of the Old Market Square are several places of interest. The Baroque **Franciscan Church** (Kościół Franciszkanów; ul. Franciszkańska 2), with its twin towers, dates from the first half of the 18th century. The interior features rich stucco work and wall paintings. Across ul. Frań-ciszkańska is the **Museum of Applied Arts** (Muzeum Sztuk Użytkowych; ul. Góra Przemysła 1; open Tues–Wed and Fri–Sat 10am–4pm, Sun 10am–3pm; admission fee), housed inside the remains of the city's former royal castle and exhibiting historical crafts such as ceramics, glass and silver. In the 13th century, a true castle stood here, but over the centuries it was continually destroyed and rebuilt. The present building, hardly a castle at all, is a reconstruction from the 18th century.

## City Centre

Further west is the **National Museum** (Muzeum Narodowe; al. Marcinkowskiego 9; open Tues 10am–6pm, Wed 9am–5pm, Thur and Sun 10am–4pm, Fri–Sat 10am–5pm; admission fee), facing Plac Wolności (Freedom Square) – which ought to be called Bank Square, given the preponderance of Polish and foreign banks here. The main building of the museum is the older one, built at the beginning of the 20th century and modelled on the Berlin Arsenal. The collection of medieval art, 16th- to 18th-century European painting – featuring Spanish and Flemish Old Masters – and contemporary Polish art by artists including Malczewski, Matejko and Wyspiański, is quite impressive. The museum's new wing, opened in 2001, isn't so new at all. It was begun in 1980, which is why, though brand new, it has a dated feel to it. It hosts visiting exhibitions.

Also on Freedom Square is the **Raczyński Library**, commissioned in the early 19th century and modelled on the Musée du Louvre in Paris. It is one of Poland's oldest public libraries.

### Croissant crazy

Poznań is famous for its celebrations on 11 November honouring the 4th-century St Martin. On that day only Poznańians gobble up St Martin croissants, in the shape of buffalo horns, stuffed with poppy seeds.

Architecture from the days of Prussian control of Poznań can be found west of Freedom Square. Look for the colon-naded **Grand Theatre** (Teatr Wielki; ul. Fredry 9), with a classical portico, and the neo-Renaissance **Collegium Minus** of the university. In front of the university is a **Monument to the Victims of Poznań, June 1956**, whose two crosses mourn the protesting workers who were killed during vio-lent demonstrations against the Communist government.

Across the street is the monolithic **Kaiserhaus,** also called 'the castle' by locals, constructed for the German Emperor Wilhelm II (he never once came to spend the night here). The massive structure now holds a cultural centre.

Directly west of here is Poznań's international fair grounds, which date from the 1920s and are the biggest and busiest in Poland. A 10-minute walk southwest, down ul. Franklina Roosevelta, past the Poznań Główny train station and just on

Golden Chapel

the other side of ul. Głogowska, is **Wilsona Park**, a green space dedicated to the US President Woodrow Wilson. Within the park is the **Palm House**, a magnificent greenhouse filled with 17,000 tropical plants and many cacti.

## Cathedral Island

Poznań has its origins on the tranquil little **Cathedral Island** (Ostrów Tumski), surrounded by the rivers Cybina and Warta and only a 15-minute walk east from the Old Market Square. Indeed, as the late Pope John Paul II once said, the island – today a hushed ecclesiastical district – is 'where Poland began'.

The island's crowning glory is its **Cathedral** (Katedra; Ostrów Tumski 17). At the beginning of the 9th century, the Piast Dynasty built a settlement and castle on the island. The actual foundations of the pre-Polish state are beneath the Cathedral, the oldest landmark on the island, dating back to 968. The main part of the church is Gothic, from the 14th and 15th centuries (the roof, twin towers and most of the interior were destroyed during World War II). The unusual arcaded gallery above the altar is purely decorative. On the left rear of the altar is the **Golden Chapel** (Złota Kaplica), a riot of ornate gold decoration from the first half of the 19th century, built as a mausoleum for the two rulers who were instrumental in building the Polish state, Mieszko I and his son, Bolesław the Brave. The chapel on the right aisle has fine 1616 frescoes on the arches; in the right rear, the Royal Chapel is where the last king buried in Poznań lies (all of the others were subsequently buried in Kraków). The Chapel of the Holy Sacrament holds the impressive Renaissance tomb of the Górka family. Along the aisles is a series of five unique bronze plates, original to the Cathedral, which were discovered in 1991 in St Petersburg's Hermitage Museum and returned to the cathedral. In the Cathedral crypt are the ancient foundations of the first church on this site, excavated in the 1950s, and an archaeological museum. Though the remains of the first two sovereigns of Poland are ostensibly buried here, there's no real proof of that fact.

## Malta

For leisure and sport, head to **Malta** – a lake and park district east of the Old Town. Lake Maltańskie is an artificial lake constructed in the 1950s, where there are frequent regattas, a beach and water sports, in addition to a year-round manmade ski slope and a summer toboggan run. The path around the lake is popular with runners and cyclists. Concerts and theatre performances are held in summer, and there are some good restaurants and one of Poznań's best hotels on the shore of the lake.

# EXCURSIONS FROM POZNAŃ

Two popular side trips from Poznań are to a castle and palace in the towns of Kórnik and Rogalin, respectively. Both can be visited by bus from Poznań, and you can go first to Kórnik and then on to Rogalin without having to go back to Poznań first. However, the visits would be much easier and less time-consuming with your own transport.

## Kórnik Castle

The **Kórnik Castle** (Zamek w Kórniku), about 20km (12 miles) to the southeast, was built by one of Poznań's richest, most powerful families, the Górkas, in the 15th century. The castle's modified appearance both inside and out was effected under the ownership of another important family, the Działyńskis, in the 1800s. The castle houses their collections of art and military regalia, as well as their original furnishings. Beautiful hardwood floors and carved wood portals are found throughout. The most surprising aspect of the interior is its Moorish Hall, based on the Alhambra in Granada, Spain. The grounds beyond the castle were established as an arboretum in the 19th century, with over 2,500 species of plants and trees.

## Rogalin Palace

**Rogalin Palace**, 13km (8 miles) west of Kórnik, is currently closed for restoration but will reopen in 2010. The 18th-century Baroque palace of Kazimierz Raczyński, the secretary of the king, it is noteworthy for its gardens and small museum. The right wing of the museum holds portraits of the Raczyński family and a mock-up of the London apartment of Edward, a diplomat. Off to the left of the main house is a gallery of 'salon paintings', including Polish artists like Wyspiański, Podkowiński and Malczewski. In the attractive English-style gardens are three massive oak trees, each about 600 years old. The trees were given the names of three dukes – Lech, Czech and Rus – who founded the Polish, Czech and Russian nations.

**Baroque Rogalin Palace**

# WHAT TO DO

From markets stalls and shopping malls to folk bands and opera, Poland offers a wealth of shopping and entertainment opportunities to suit all tastes and budgets. This chapter surveys some of the many options available to the visitor.

## SHOPPING

The demise of Communism in 1989 and the move to a free-market economy have had a dramatic impact on Poland as a shopping destination. Drab state-owned stores are a thing of the past. The pound, dollar, euro and other currencies don't go as far today as they once did, but foreign visitors and their Polish counterparts can only be pleased with the opening of trade and vastly improved selection of goods on the market. In major cities like Warsaw and Kraków, Poland doesn't lag far behind Western Europe and North America for commercial opportunities. Even with the end of Communism and inflation, Poland remains considerably cheaper than Western European destinations.

### Where to Shop

Poland's development of a market economy has produced a proliferation of stores and boutiques, including many imported from Western Europe and North America. You can now buy most Western goods in large and modern department stores, specialty shops and market stalls.

For folk art and other handicrafts, start at branches of Cepelia stores, a national

**Haggle ye not**

Note that the price displayed is the price that is expected to be paid — it is not the done thing to haggle in Polish shops.

chain of folk art and souvenir shops in large cities. (Occasionally, they go by different names, even though locals invariably call them Cepelia.) For antiques, the dominant player is the Desa chain (though there are many smaller, independent dealers as well). In Kraków and Warsaw there are a few branches, each with different stock, so it pays to visit a few if you're looking for a particular item. There are essentially three places in the country for Polish poster art: in Kraków, Galeria Plakatu Kraków (ul. Stolarska 8–10); and in Warsaw, Galeria Plakatu (ul. Hoża 40) and the Poster Museum (Muzeum Plakatu) at Wilanów Palace.

Speciality shopping markets and unique venues exist in several cities. These include the famous, long-established **Cloth Hall stalls**, loaded with crafts and amber jewellery, in Kraków; Warsaw's swank, boutique-lined **ul. Nowy Świat**; and **ul. Mariacka** in Gdańsk's Main Town for amber jewellery. An interesting open-air market in Warsaw is the Koło Bazaar, in Wola. In Kraków, the traders' market is between the train station and the Barbican. In Gdańsk, the covered market (Hala Targowa) is at pl. Dominikański 1.

Good sources for local shops and markets in Warsaw, Kraków and Gdańsk are the local editions of the *In Your Pocket* guide, which features individual store listings. See

## Amber

This attractive fossilised tree resin (not a semi-precious stone) is available in many shades, from yellow to brown, and grades of clarity. The cities near the Baltic Sea, Gdańsk and Gdynia, have an abundance of amber and excellent shops, often dealing in unique pieces. Be careful not to buy amber on the street, as it is likely to be fake; look for a sign of the Amber Association of Poland ('Societas Svccinorvm in Polonia') in shop windows as a guarantee of quality and authenticity.

<www.inyourpocket.com> for more information.

Bargaining is generally only acceptable at the large **open-air markets**, though if you ask for a discount at an antiques store or art gallery, you may well be granted one.

## What to Buy

**Art & antiques.** You'll find excellent antique furnishings and religious art throughout Poland, though the best pieces tend to wind up in the wide spectrum of shops and galleries in Warsaw and Kraków, and to a lesser extent cities like Gdańsk and Poznań. Reli-

Baltic amber for sale in Gdańsk

gious icons from the Orthodox Church in Russia can be found, as a large black market in stolen icons exists throughout Central and Eastern Europe, although officials are understandably touchy about their export, even when the item in question is not originally from Poland.

**Ceramics & pottery.** Distinctive Kashubian pottery known as Ceramika Artystyczna Bolesławiec is sold the world over but is considerably cheaper in Poland.

**Folk art.** Rustic Poland excels at folk art and handicrafts, including hand-carved wooden (usually religious) figures; leather goods from the Tatra Mountains; embroidery and lace; hand-painted eggs (especially at Easter); and colourful naïve art and glass paintings, especially that of Zakopane.

**Music.** CDs from Polish composers are available in record shops in major cities. The most recognisable to Western listeners are probably composers Chopin, Krzysztof Penderecki and Henryk Górecki, who unexpectedly scored an international best seller with his Symphony No. 3 in the early 1990s. A contemporary film composer, Zbigniew Preisner, who wrote the scores for the Polish director Krzysztof Kieślowski's films, including *The Double Life of Veronique*, *Dekalogue* and the *Three Colours* trilogy: *Red*, *White* and *Blue*, is worth seeking out. Of special note is a recording of the best

Wickerwork is a speciality

of Preisner recorded live in the Wieliczka Salt Mines outside Kraków. You can also find recordings of Polish folk music, such as traditional *górale* tunes from the Tatras.

**Poster art.** Poster design is a thriving and valued art form in Poland, and some of the finest poster artists in the world are Polish. You'll find vintage and contemporary posters for familiar Western films and the greatest hits of theatre and opera, as well as more obscure titles. Contemporary poster designers include Górowsky, Stasys and Sadowski.

**Vodka.** For an authentic bottle of Polish vodka, or *wódka* (pronounced 'voot-ka'), look for Wyborowa, Extra Żytnia or any flavoured vodka, such as Żubrówka (with a blade of bison grass in the bottle) and Wiśniówka (cherry-flavoured).

# ENTERTAINMENT

Nightlife in Warsaw and Kraków is very cosmopolitan, with a full range of cultural offerings, including theatre, opera, ballet and classical music. In other cities, there is less variety, though both Gdańsk and Poznań have healthy schedules of fine arts. Tickets for performances are much more accessibly priced than in most of Western Europe and in North America.

On the pop culture front, you'll find jazz combos and films from around the world. Big-name international pop and rock bands make only occasional appearances in Poland. You'll find a range of bars, pubs, cafés and nightclubs in the cities, as well as a handful of casinos.

**Performing arts.** In the principal cities, Poles are stalwart supporters of the performing arts. In Warsaw, the Great Theatre – National Opera (pl. Teatralny 1, tel: 022 826 5019, <www.teatrwielki.pl>) is the foremost venue in Poland for opera and ballet; Kiri Te Kanawa, Kathleen Battle and José Carreras have all sung here. For classical music concerts, the National Philharmonic Hall (ul. Jasna 5, tel: 022 551 7131, <www.filharmonia.pl>) and the intimate Opera Kameralna (al. Solidarności 76b, tel: 022 831 2240, <www.opera kameralna.pl>) are among the nation's best. There are also occasional concerts at the Royal Castle on pl. Zamkowy (tel: 022 657 2170). In Kraków, Juliusz Słowacki Theatre (pl. Św. Ducha 1, tel: 012 423 1700, <www. slowacki.krakow.pl>) is the venue for opera, as well as theatre and concerts; for the-

Kraków's Słowacki Theatre

atre and dance, Operetta Stage (ul. Lubicz 48, tel: 012 421 4200); and for music events, the Philharmonic Hall (ul. Zwierzyniecka 1, tel: 012 429 1345, <www.filharmonia. krakow.pl>). Concerts are also held at St Mary's Cathedral, SS Peter & Paul Church on Wawel Hill and in summer at the Chopin Monument in Warsaw's Łazienki Park. In Gdańsk, the State Baltic Opera (Al. Zwycięstwa 15, tel: 058 763 4906, <www.operabaltycka.pl>) is one of the best in Poland, holding opera and symphonic concerts, while chamber music concerts are held at the Baltic Philharmonic Hall (Ołowianka 1, tel: 058 320 6262, <www.filharmonia. gda.pl>). In Poznań, opera is performed at the Teatr Wielki (ul. Fredry 9, tel: 061 659 0200, <www.opera.poznan.pl>) and classical music at Filharmonia Poznańska (ul. Św. Marcina 81, tel: 061 852 4708, <www.filharmoniapoznanska.pl>). Poznań is also well known for its acclaimed ballet company, the Polish Dance Theatre-Poznań Ballet (ul. Kozia 4, tel: 061 852 4242, <www.ptt-poznan.pl>).

Drama is staged almost entirely in Polish, tending to exclude most foreign tourists. Acting and directing are of a very high standard, though, and adventurous theatregoers who don't mind not understanding the language in order to see first-rate acting and production will find plenty of excellent performances, especially in Kraków, the epicentre of the Polish theatre world. The Stary Teatr, or Old Theatre (ul. Jagiellońska 1, tel: 012 422 4040, <www.stary-teatr.pl>) is the top venue, with a main stage and two ancillary stages. In Warsaw, top musicals of the

**In your pocket**

For schedules of opera and classical music concerts, see the local editions of the English-language publication *In Your Pocket*, <www.inyourpocket.com>, which contain good round-ups of nightlife in Warsaw, Kraków and Gdańsk, and *Warsaw Insider*, a free monthly publication for Warsaw.

Music bar in Kraków's main square

Andrew Lloyd Webber variety land at Roma (ul. Nowo-grodzka 49, tel: 022 628 0360).

**Cinema.** Poland has an enviable cinematic tradition and has produced great film directors who've gone on to international success, including Krzysztof Kieślowski, Andrzej Wajda and Roman Polański. Poles are dedicated moviegoers, so in the cities you'll find plenty of subtitled Western films on the marquees competing with home-grown product, showing at good, Dolby sound-equipped cinemas. Film admissions are cheap by comparison with many countries. Look out for the Warsaw Film Festival in October every year.

**Clubs and bars.** Poland's towns and cities teem with bars, pubs and clubs, and Poles are known as heavy drinkers. The days of hard-drinking men emptying bottles of vodka in poorly lit bars are largely a thing of the past, though, and most Poles today drink more beer *(piwo)* than vodka and other spirits. You'll find Irish and English pubs and nightclubs across Poland.

Bars in atmospheric cellars, and others above ground, have proliferated in recent years in Kraków's Old Town. With so many students in town, they're usually packed. There are so many it is difficult to single out only a few, but among the most interesting are: Black Gallery (ul. Mikołajska 24); Free Pub (ul. Sławkowska 4); Stalowe Magnolie (ul. Św. Jana 15), which has live music and boudoir-style backrooms; U Louisa (Rynek Główny 13); Bastylia (ul. Stolarska 3); and Alchemia (ul. Estery 5) and Singer Café (ul. Estery 22), in Kazimierz. The distinction between cafés and bars is sometimes difficult to ascertain, but some of the many excellent cafés in Kraków include: Camelot (ul. Św. Tomasza 17), Dym (ul. Św. Tomasza 13), Jama Michalika (ul. Floriańska 45) and Wiśniowy Sad (ul. Grodzka 33). For jazz and blues clubs in Kraków, try U Muniaka (ul. Floriańska 3), Klub Indigo (ul. Floriańska 26) and Klinika 35 (ul. Św. Tomasza 35).

Warsaw doesn't have quite as appealing a cluster of bars in one pub-crawl-ready area, but the capital certainly has its share of watering holes and cafés. It has a mini collection of Irish pubs, including Morgan's (ul. Okólnik 1, downstairs from the Chopin Museum), Irish Pub (ul. Miodowa 3) and Cork Irish Pub (Al. Niepodległości 19). Other bars are Lolek (ul. Rokitnicka 20), the elegant Column Bar in the Hotel Bristol (ul. Krakowskie Przedmieście 42–4). For cocktails try Paparazi (ul. Mazowiecka 12). Nightclubs include Ground Zero (ul. Wspólna 62), Quo Vadis (Pl. Defilad 1), and for jazz and blues Jazz Café Helicon (ul. Freta 45–7) and Jazz Bistro (ul. Piękna 20).

Gdańsk has a lively roster of pubs in its Main Town. The coolest are Latający Holender (ul. Wały Jagiellońskie 2-4) and Vinifera (ul. Wodopój 7) for wines by the glass. For live jazz, check out Cotton Club (ul. Złotników 25) and Jazz Club (Długi Targ 39–40).

Skiing on Mt Kasprowy Wierch in the Tatras

## SPORTS

The most popular sport in Poland, as in most European nations, is football (soccer), although other sports including ice hockey, volleyball, wind surfing and skiing are also popular. Poland hasn't yet developed much as a sport-specific destination. That said, the countryside is ideal for outdoor enthusiasts, and even though most of those destinations are beyond the scope of this guide, visitors interested in horse-riding, skiing, fishing and hiking have myriad options.

**Golf.** If you've just got to play golf on your business trip to Warsaw, head for the First Warsaw Golf and Country Club (Rajszew 70, Jabłonna, tel: 022 782 4555, <www.warsaw golf.pl>), an 18-hole course about 30km (19 miles) outside of the capital. Perhaps the best golfing is near the Baltic Sea, at the Postołów Golf Club (Postołow, tel: 058 683 7100, <www.golf.com.pl>), 26km (16 miles) south of Gdańsk.

**Hiking and walking.** The vast countryside of Poland is ideal for leisurely walking and more athletic hiking. One of the best areas for both, especially for serious hikers, are the High Tatra Mountains around Zakopane.

**Horse-riding.** Equestrian holidays are becoming increasingly popular in Poland; ask your travel agent about Orbis horse-riding holidays. If you just want to get in the saddle a time or two, contact Pa-ta-Taj Horse-Riding School (Szkoła Jazdy Konnej, ul. Krótka 9, tel: 022 758 5835) in Warsaw. There are a couple of dozen stables and riding schools in

Windsurfing on Hel Peninsula

the environs of the capital; ask for additional information from tourist information centres or your hotel.

**Skiing.** The hotspot for skiing is Zakopane, at the foot of the High Tatra Mountains in southeastern Poland. Skiing is excellent, inexpensive and very popular with Poles and some foreign vacationers on ski packages, even though facilities lag behind resorts in the Alps and Pyrenees.

**Swimming and water sports.** In Warsaw, the Victoria, Marriott and Bristol hotels have swimming pools. Less ritzy are these pools: Aquapark Wesolandia (ul. Wspólna 4, tel: 022 773 9191, <www.wesolandia.pl>), Polna (ul. Polna 7a, tel: 022 825 71 34, <www.osir-polna.pl>) and Wodny Park (ul. Merliniego 4, tel: 022 854 0130, <www.wodnypark.com.pl>).

Kraków also has several pools open to visitors: Park Wodny (ul. Dobrego Pasterza 126, tel: 012 616 3190, <www.park wodny.pl>), Copernicus (ul. Kanonicza 16, tel: 012 424 3400) and Sheraton (ul. Powiśle 7, tel: 012 662 1000).

The vast majority of boating and other water sports is concentrated in the Mazurian Lakes district in northeastern Poland and the towns along the Bay of Gdańsk, on the Baltic Sea.

## Spectator Sports

**Football.** Football (soccer) is Poland's most popular spectator sport. Warsaw's two first-division football teams are Legia Warszawa (ul. Łazienkowska 3, tel: 022 628 4303, <www.legialive.pl>) and Polonia Warszawa (ul. Konwiktorska 6, tel: 022 635 1637, <www.ksppolonia.com>).

# CHILDREN

Travelling with children in Poland is a matter of being flexible, creative, and putting together activities to keep the kids interested when palaces, castles and rebuilt old towns impress them less than they do their parents. Many of the activities listed below are in the capital, Warsaw, where there is simply a greater abundance of facilities.

Warsaw Zoo (ul. Ratuszowa 1–3, tel: 022 619 4041, <www.zoo.waw.pl>) has been open since 1928. The habitats of some 4,000 animals, including Siberian tigers, kangaroos, cheetahs, crocodiles, snow leopards and an unusual red panda, are spread across 40 hectares (99 acres). The zoo also has a free-flight bird hall. Entertainment Park Pepeland (ul. Kolejowa 378, tel: 022 751 2627) also has a mini zoo and various rides.

Another option for kids in Warsaw is the Teatr Guliwer (ul. Różana 16, tel: 022 845 1677, <www.teatrguliwer.waw.pl>).

For children with energy to burn, there are water parks and swimming pools *(see above)* in summer, and ice rinks in win-

Children may like Polish bison

ter. To go ice skating, check out the Stegny (ul. Inspektowa 1, tel: 022 842 2768, <www.stegny.com.pl>) or Towarzystwo Łyżwiarstwa Figurowego Walley (ul. Kombatantów 60, Julianów, tel: 022 711 1261, <www.walley.pl>) in Warsaw. Another activity that is all the rage is paintball: in Warsaw, try Marcus-Graf (ul. Widok 10, in Beniaminów near Warsaw, tel: 022 816 1008) or Paintballs Club (ul. Lokajskiego 42, tel: 060 266 9220, <www.paintballs-club.pl>). Paintballers in Kraków should check out Compass (tel: 012 357 3370, <www.compass-poland.com>), the local experts who provide a number of other activities including 4x4 off-roading and the inevitable stag weekend pranks.

Another fast-paced sport is go-karts. In Warsaw, race the kids over to Imola, where they also have paintball (ul. Puławska 33, Piaseczno, tel: 022 757 0823, <www.imola.pl>). If your kids like bowling, you'll find facilities in all the major cities. In the Malta lake district of Poznań, there are many facilities ideal for children, including a man-made ski slope and a exhilarating toboggan run.

For older kids who enjoy hiking and skiing, the area around Zakopane in the Tatra Mountains is the best in Poland. Sure to be cool for kids are the 700-year-old Wieliczka Salt Mines near Kraków *(see pages 55–7)*, where you first descend 378 steps, then continue through long corridors and see chapels and figures (including the Seven Dwarves) entirely carved out of salt, and finally zoom up to ground level via a fast and slightly shaky bare-bones elevator.

## Festivals and Events

**February** International Festival of Sailors' Songs (Shanties), Warsaw
**March/April** Holy Week religious celebrations, all Poland
**March** Poznań Jazz Festival, Poznań
**April** Festival of Contemporary Music, Poznań
**April/May** Warsaw Ballet Days, Warsaw
**May** Music and Art Festival, Toruń
International Book Fair, Warsaw
Jazz Festival, Poznań
**June** International Theatre Festival, Poznań
Summer Jazz Days, Warsaw
Jewish Culture Festival, Kraków
Midsummer's Night celebrations, Kraków
**24 June** St John's Feast Day, especially in Warsaw, Kraków and Poznań
**June/July** Mozart Festival, Warsaw
Theatre Summer Festival, Zamość
**July** Summer Festival of Early Music, Kraków
Summer Festival of Opera, Kraków
Organ Music Festival, Gdańsk
**July/August** Dominican Fair, Gdańsk
**August** International Song Festival, Sopot
International Festival of Old Music, Kraków
International Festival of Highland Folklore, Zakopane
International Chopin Festival, Duszniki Zdrój, near Wroclaw
**September** International Violin Makers Competition, Poznań
**October** Chopin International Piano Competition (held in Warsaw every 5 years; next in 2010)
Warsaw Film Festival, Warsaw
International Jazz Festival, Warsaw
**November** All Saints' Day
All Saints' Day Jazz Festival, Kraków
Warsaw Ancient Music Festival, Warsaw
**December** Most Beautiful Nativity Crib Contest, Kraków (Rynek)

# EATING OUT

Polish cuisine ranges from light and elegant to rich and hearty, invariably served in generous portions. Soups are a speciality, while potatoes and dumplings are a staple, and vegetables are available in a variety of dishes. Given its shifting borders over the centuries, it's not surprising that Polish cooking also shows the influence of several national cuisines, namely Ukrainian, German, Lithuanian and Russian.

People in other countries are frequently familiar with certain items common in the Polish diet, including *pierogi* (stuffed dumplings), *barszcz* (beetroot soup) and *kiełbasa* (Polish sausage), as well as the ubiquitous menu items like herrings, charcuterie or sauerkraut. Probably the most traditional Polish dish is *bigos* ('hunter's stew'), a sauerkraut

Inside Café Larousse, Kraków

dish laced with several meats (pork, game, sausage, bacon and more).

The restaurant scene in Poland, like almost everything else, has changed dramatically in the years since the fall of the Communist regime. Eating out, at least as far as fine dining was concerned, used to be a rarity, and shortages and rationing were common. No longer. Restaurants of all styles have blossomed in major towns, though tradi-

Café Huśtawka sign, Kraków

tional restaurants serving classic Polish cuisine have not disappeared, thankfully. They should be the focus of any visitor's dining habits in Poland.

## WHERE TO EAT

Most visitors will eat the majority of their meals in a *restauracja* (restaurant). These range from inexpensive eateries, where office workers take their lunch, to upmarket dining rooms frequented far more by foreign visitors and a small handful of elite Poles than by ordinary citizens; restaurants have table service.

A café *(kawiarnia)* is not strictly a coffeehouse. Most also have a menu and serve everything from snacks to full meals at all hours of the day. Another traditional eatery is the cheap, cafeteria-style, self-service creature called a *bar mleczny*, literally a milk bar. Often you can get a good, home-cooked and filling plate for very little.

Dining in Kraków

## WHEN TO EAT

In Poland breakfast *(śniadanie)* is generally served between the hours of 7 and 10am. Poles typically eat bread or a roll served with butter, cheese, and ham or sausage. Eggs for breakfast are not uncommon. At most upmarket hotels, a basic international breakfast buffet will generally be served. Often you will find local pastries and possibly some foods you may not think of as usual breakfast fare.

Lunch *(obiad)*, generally served between 2 and 4pm, is traditionally the main meal of the day, a fact reflected in the quantities that are served at this time of day. The obiad typically consists of three courses: soup, main course and dessert.

Dinner *(kolacja)* is served early evening, and it can either be similar to and nearly as substantial as the *obiad* or considerably lighter, with a similar selection to what would be served for breakfast.

# POLISH COOKING

Certain ingredients are essential to traditional Polish cuisine: fish, game, potatoes, wild mushrooms and other vegetables. One of the most distinctive flavours of Polish cooking is sourness, but it can also be hot or sweet.

Some traditional dishes are cooked in lard, although oil or butter is the norm for most dishes. If portions are too hefty for you, order soup and then an appetiser instead of a main, and try to leave room for dessert.

The undisputed Polish folk dish is *pierogi*, which are originally from Russia and date back to medieval times. *Pierogi* can be sweet or savoury. Ravioli-like dumplings are filled with a variety of stuffings, including fresh cabbage or sauerkraut mixed with mushrooms; cheese and potatoes; or fruits in summer. Small *pierogi* are sometimes served in soups. Stuffed cabbage is another traditional dish, the leaves are filled with minced meat and rice, and usually served with tomato sauce. Poles are also very fond of potato pancakes and potato dumplings.

On menus in restaurants, main courses frequently do not include accompaniments. Potatoes, salads and other side dishes are listed under *dodatki* and served at additional cost.

*Oscypek,* a smoked cheese, is a Zakopane speciality

## Soup

Soup *(zupa)* is immensely popular with locals and always on the menu. Most Poles think a meal incomplete without soup (some

## Toilet tip

In public toilets, the men's room is often indicated by a triangle, while the women's is shown by a circle.

visitors may find Polish soups, on the other hand, to be complete meals). *Barszcz czerwony* (red beetroot soup) is an ancient recipe; the authentic version has a distinctive taste. It can be served clear or with cream and with small ravioli-like dumplings. Beetroot soup made with vegetable stock and served with mushroom-filled *uszka* (small ravioli) is traditional for Christmas Eve. *Żurek*, or white *barszcz*, is made from rye flour then fermented, before being seasoned. It is sometimes served with sausage or a hardboiled egg. *Chłodnik* is a cold beetroot summer soup which includes thick soured cream combined with cucumbers, radishes, chives and dill. *Ogórkowa* (dill cucumber soup) is also sour, as is *kapuśniak* (sauerkraut soup). Other soups to enjoy are *grzybowa* (mushroom soup), *szczawiowa*, or sorrel soup, and *zupa koperkowa*, which features the national herb, dill.

## Starters

The classic starter *(przekąski)* is herring, which can be served in various ways. They are often served in oil, or with soured cream, or with lots of chopped onions. Poland also produces a broad range of sausages and hams, which are a speciality and a national favourite of Poles. You'll also find jellied carp, pike and smoked eel as appetisers, as well as smaller portions of favourite main courses, such as *pierogi* or potato pancakes.

## Main Courses

**Meat (*mięso; dania mięsne*).** Poland is a nation of avid carnivores, and to most Poles, a meal of substance includes meat. Pork is by far the most popular meat dish. The classic preparation is a pork cutlet prepared with fried onions, coated in bread crumbs and served with stewed cabbage. Roast pork is eaten both hot and cold. Hot pot roast may be served with dried prunes. Beef is less common, though *zrazy zawijane* (beef rolls filled with bacon, dark bread and mushrooms) is a standard dish. *Flaki po polsku* (tripe stew) is thin strips of beef tripe, boiled in meat and vegetable stock and served with dark bread. The meat dish not to be missed in Poland is *bigos*, a classic hunter's preparation. It is fresh cabbage and sauerkraut, often stewed with a number of different types of meat and sausage (meat and cabbage in equal proportion). It is the supreme Polish winter meal.

**Game *(dziczyzna)* and poultry *(drób)*.** Game is very popular, as you might expect from the national affinity for meat and rich tastes. Venison *(sarna)* is usually reserved for elite restaurants, as are wild boar *(dzik)* and other 'exotic' game. Look, too, for hare *(zając)* and pheasant *(bażant)*. Chicken *(kura)* is popular and is typically stuffed and roasted. Chicken soup is another great Polish favourite, as is roasted duck *(kaczka)* with apples.

**Fish *(dania rybne)*.** Fish is as popular on menus as pork and other meats, with pike, eel, perch, sturgeon and others – boiled, fried or roasted – found in most good restaurants. Carp is a particular

Hearty, healthy Polish cuisine – heavy on the beets

favourite (especially on Christmas Eve), often served in aspic or Polish sauce with raisins and almonds.

**Vegetables** *(potrawy jarskie)*. Vegetarian restaurants are now much less of a rarity in Poland, though classic milk bars began basically as vegetarian places, most having now added a few meat dishes. Vegetable accompaniments usually have to be ordered separately and can be very creative. Vegetarians should steer towards potato pancakes or dumplings stuffed with fruit, *pierogi* filled with cheese and potato, and crepes. Salads include tomato salads, sliced cucumbers in sour cream, and sauerkraut.

## Desserts

Poles are great eaters of pastries and sweets. Among those you're likely to find on menus and fellow diners' plates are *eklerka* (éclairs), *napoleonki* (millefeuille), *sernik* (cheesecake), *szarlotka* (apple tarts) and traditional *mazurek* – thin flat cakes topped with nuts and fruits.

### The National Spirit

The Poles and Russians may bicker about who created it, but vodka (wódka) is a staple of the Polish diet. Most vodkas are distilled from rye, but a few are made from potatoes – both types have a distinct character. It is usually clear, though you'll also find coloured and flavoured versions. Wyborowa (distilled from rye) is the standard-bearer, with a range of flavoured vodkas also produced under the brand name; look also for Luksusowa (distilled from potatoes) and Żubrówka (which is flavoured with bison grass from the Białowieża forest), and kosher vodkas.

Vodka is heavily ritualised. If you visit someone at home, it's polite to take a bottle, though you're not expected to empty it. Poles drink vodka neat – either in one gulp or sipped – rather than in cocktails (though Tatanka, Żubrówka vodka with apple juice, is popular).

# DRINKS

Poland does not produce grape wine. Imported wines are available in cafés and restaurants; the cheaper varieties are Hungarian and Bulgarian. You'll also find French, Italian and Spanish wines, but be prepared to pay for the privilege.

Vodka, the Polish national spirit, usually drunk neat

Polish beers, or *piwo*, go well with heavy, spicy foods; except at the most formal of restaurants, it is as acceptable to drink beer with a meal as it is wine. Polish beers, usually served in tall glasses, are generally light and drinkable, although they do not enjoy the same reputation as their Czech, German, Belgian or English counterparts. Among the best-known brands are Żywiec, Okocim, EB, Warka and Tyskie. For information on brewery tours and the Brewing Museum at the Tyskie Brewery in Tychy, 20km (12 miles) south of Katowice, see <www.kp.pl>.

Coffee *(kawa)* is a favourite drink of Poles and is usually served black (unless you ask for milk) or with a just a dash of milk. Espresso and capuccino are widely available. Tea *(herbata)*, usually served with lemon, is drunk by most Poles.

International soft drinks and mineral water *(woda mineralna)* are readily available.

Stylish bar in Kraków

## Menu Reader

| | | | |
|---|---|---|---|
| **barszcz** | beetroot soup | **mięso** | meat |
| **befsztyk** | beef steak | **ogórek** | cucumber |
| **bigos** | sauerkraut and meat dish | **piwo** | beer |
| | | **polędwica** | beef |
| **chleb** | bread | **ryba** | fish |
| **frytki** | chips/fries | **ryż** | rice |
| **gołąbki** | stuffed cabbage leaves | **sałatka** | salad |
| | | **ser** | cheese |
| **golonka** | boiled pork knuckle | **szynka** | ham |
| | | **woda** | water |
| **grzyb** | mushroom | **wódka** | vodka |
| **herbata** | tea | **ziemniaki** | potatoes |
| **jarzyny** | vegetables | **zrazy** | stuffed beef rolls |
| **kawa** | coffee | | |
| **kotlet** | fried pork cutlet | **zupa** | soup |
| **kurczak** | chicken | **żurek** | rye-flour soup |

# HANDY TRAVEL TIPS

An A–Z Summary of Practical Information

# A

## ACCOMMODATION

Hotels in Poland are unofficially graded from one star to five stars, and those rating three to five are of comparable international standard. In smaller cities, there is a shortage of good hotels; but there is a growing number of good three-star hotels and a few two- or one-star hotels that can be recommended. Warsaw, Kraków and other larger cities have an increasing number of top-flight, five-star hotels targeting business travellers and upmarket tourists. The Orbis chain used to have a virtual monopoly on mid- and top-level hotels; this is no longer the case, as international chains and independents have increased the competition.

| | |
|---|---|
| Do you have a room? | **Czy sà wolne pokoje?** |
| How much is it? | **Ile kosztuje?** |
| single | **pojedynczy pokój** |
| double | **podwójny pokój** |
| without bath / with bath | **bez łazienki / z łazienkà** |
| expensive | **drogi** |

If all the higher grade hotels are full, or beyond your budget, the best option is to stay slightly out of town in a pension or guesthouse hotel. Other options are accommodation in private homes or a self-catering apartment. Accommodation in private homes *(kwatery prywatne)* is common throughout Poland. There are also more than 200 registered campsites and a network of youth hostels in the major cities.

It is essential to book ahead during peak season (May to October). Tourism Information Offices (including the one at the airport) will provide lists of accommodation.

Room prices, which should be posted at the reception desk, usually include VAT and often but not always include breakfast. Outside of the most expensive hotels, prices are generally lower than those in other European countries. Confusingly, hotels may list their prices in US dollars, euros or Polish złoty.

## AIRPORTS *(lotnisko)*

**Warsaw:** International flights arrive and depart from Okęcie International Airport, south of the capital. There are car-hire agencies, left luggage, money exchange desks, cash machines, travel agents, a restaurant and a tourist information office. It takes about 30 minutes to get from the airport to the centre of Warsaw. A taxi will cost between 25 zł and 80 zł (more at night) depending on which one you choose. Some of the taxis waiting out front may look official, but are not and will cheat you as much as they can.

If you need to take a taxi, call for one at the information desk: Halo Taxi (tel: 022 9623), MPT (tel: 022 9191) or Super Taxi (tel: 022 9622). By bus (5am to 10.30pm), take No. 175 or 188 to the city centre (watch out for pickpockets); the bus stops at all red bus stops and Centralna train station. Some hotels operate a shuttle-bus service to and from the airport. Airport Information, tel: 022 650 4220.

**Kraków:** Balice Airport, also known as John Paul II International Airport, is 18km west of town. To get to Kraków, take a taxi; call Barbakan Taxi (tel: 012 9661) or Mega Taxi (tel: 012 9625). Prices range from around 40–60 zł. Alternatively, take bus no. 192, which goes to the Old Town and train station. Airport information, tel: 012 639 3000. You can catch a free bus from outside the main international terminal doors to a platform from which a train runs direct to the city's central train station. Journey time is 15 minutes, and tickets cost 8zł.

**Gdańsk:** Flights from London and a handful of other European cities (Hamburg, Copenhagen, Brussels) land at Port Lotniczy Gdańsk Trójmiasto, less than 10km (6 miles) west of the city centre. A taxi will cost between 30 and 40 zł; call City Plus (tel: 058 9686) or Servis Taxi (tel: 058 9194) for pickup rather than taking a waiting unofficial cab. Bus B goes from the airport to the main train station in Gdańsk (40 minutes). Airport information, tel: 058 348 1111.

## B

### BUDGETING FOR YOUR TRIP

Though prices have risen dramatically in the past few years, Poland remains inexpensive for most visitors from Western Europe and North America, relative to other European countries. Still, visitors expecting the dirt-cheap Central Europe of the very recent past may be in for a bit of a surprise. Four- and five-star hotels in Warsaw and Kraków are now nearly as costly as those in Western Europe. However, many facets of daily life remain true bargains for visitors: the highly efficient public transport system, restaurants and cafés, and museums and concert performances.

**Transport to Poland.** For most Europeans, Warsaw or Kraków is a short, fairly inexpensive flight or train ride away. North Americans (and of course Australians, New Zealanders and South Africans) can expect their flights to eat up considerably more of their budgets – anywhere from US$700 to US$1,000 or more, though off-season roundtrip deals on Polish LOT from New York and Canada can sometimes be had for as little as US$500. A growing number of budget carriers also offer very competitive prices.

**Accommodation.** Confusingly, hotels may list their prices in US dollars, euros or Polish złoty. Top hotels are close if not equal to what you might expect to find in other European capital cities. Approximate price of a double room in high season, in central Warsaw or Kraków: 5-star hotel 500–1,000 zł (US$125–250); 3- to 4-star hotel 200–400 zł (US$50–100); 2-star hotel or pension 40–150 zł (US$10–40).

**Meals and drinks.** Dining out in Poland remains a bargain except at the most upmarket and famous restaurants. A three-course meal for two people, with wine and service, in a moderately priced restaurant can cost about 80 zł (US$25); at an expensive restaurant, 160 zł (US$50) or more.

**Local transport.** Public transport is inexpensive whether bus, Metro (subway) or tram (2.4–4 zł). Only taxis are relatively expensive (especially if you wind up in an unofficial taxi). Opt for public transport except in rare instances (after-hours), and always call for a taxi rather than hail one on the street.

**Incidentals.** Car hire is expensive: daily rates in US$, including unlimited mileage, range from $70–100/day for an economy-size car, including CDW insurance. At press time, petrol (gas) cost 4.20 zł per litre. Museum admission: around 4 zł. Entertainment: theatre, musicals and classical music concerts generally start from 20 zł.

## C

## CAR HIRE

Hiring a car in Poland isn't a great idea unless you intend to explore the countryside in considerable depth. Car hire is expensive (US$70–100/day), and the road network in Poland leaves much to be desired; roads are in need of repair and few motorways exist (there isn't one between Warsaw and Kraków). Arrangements and conditions for car hire are similar to those in other countries. The minimum age requirement is 21 and you must have been in possession of a valid licence for at least one year. US and Canadian licences are accepted as are international driving licences.

Ask if CDW insurance is included in the price. There are a few local agencies, such as Global Poland (Warsaw, tel: 022 650 1483), which tend to be cheaper, in addition to the major international agencies, including: Avis (Warsaw, tel: 022 650 4872; Kraków, tel: 060 120 0702; <www.avis.pl>), Budget (Warsaw, tel: 022 650 4062), Europcar (Warsaw, tel: 022 650 2564; Kraków, tel: 012 633 7773), Hertz (Warsaw, tel: 022 650 2896; Kraków, tel: 012 429 6262), and Sixt (Warsaw, tel: 022 650 2031; Kraków, tel: 012 639 3216).

| Where's the nearest petrol (gas) station? | Gdzie jest najbliższa stacja benzynowa? |

## CLIMATE

All of Poland is very cold in winter, and warm but comfortable in summer (it can sometimes be very hot). The best weather (and time to visit) is from May to early June and September to October. Temperatures in the highlands around Zakopane are very cold in winter. The chart below shows the average daytime temperature for Warsaw, in degrees Celsius and Fahrenheit:

|      | J  | F  | M  | A  | M  | J  | J  | A  | S  | O  | N  | D  |
|------|----|----|----|----|----|----|----|----|----|----|----|----|
| °C   | -1 | -2 | 3  | 12 | 15 | 18 | 17 | 18 | 12 | 12 | 6  | 1  |
| °F   | 30 | 28 | 37 | 54 | 59 | 64 | 63 | 64 | 54 | 54 | 43 | 34 |

## CLOTHING

Poles in the big cities – especially Warsaw and Kraków – tend to be style-conscious, and chic Western fashions are very much in evidence. A jacket and tie would only be suggested at special theatre or opera occasions or very exclusive restaurants. Clothing in the countryside is usually informal.

## CRIME AND SAFETY

Crime has risen considerably in Polish cities, and Warsaw cannot be considered a safe place. As far as visitors are concerned, the major crime is pickpocketing (usually on buses and trams) or car theft. Take the usual precautions, especially on trips to and from the airport and the railway station, and at night. Assaults are not unheard of, and drug-related crimes are a particular danger.

Other cities, including Kraków, are generally safer, though always be careful in areas frequented by tourists (Wawel Hill, Market Square). The tri-city area of Gdańsk, Gdynia and Sopot has a high incidence of muggings, sometimes in broad daylight.

Organised groups of thieves and pickpockets sometimes operate at major tourist destinations, in railway stations and on trains, trams and buses in major cities. Thefts have occurred on overnight trains, especially in second-class closed compartments, though the most common occurrence is when boarding. Car thefts, car-jackings and theft from cars are commonplace. If driving, do not pull over if another driver intimates that something is wrong with your car; it is very likely a set-up for a robbery. There are also reports of thieves opening or breaking passenger-side doors and windows in slow or stopped traffic.

## CUSTOMS AND ENTRY REQUIREMENTS

All visitors require a valid passport to enter Poland (it must be valid for three months after the date of departure). The citizens of many countries, including most European nations, Australia, New Zealand, Canada and the US, do not need a visa. However, citizens of South Africa require visas. Valid for 90 days, visas can be obtained from any Polish diplomatic mission; this usually takes 24 hours.

**Customs restrictions.** There is no limit on the amount of foreign currency that can be brought into Poland, though excessive amounts should be declared at customs upon arrival. The export of antiques and works of art created before 1945 is prohibited; works of art produced by living artists after 1945 may be exported with permission from the National Museum/Provincial Conservator of Relics (so too can some pre-1945 works if the National Museum judges them not to be 'of museum quality'). Certain works of art produced after 1945 may still be subject to a ban on exportation if the artist is no longer living and the work is deemed of high cultural value.

Those who wish to export a pre-1945 artwork must get a document certifying such by the National Museum Department of Art Certification (Dział Opinionwania Dzieł Sztuki), ul. Myśli-wiecka 1, Warsaw. For customs questions, tel: 022 694 3194, <www.mf.gov.pl>.

## D

### DRIVING

To take your car into Poland you need a valid driving licence and car registration papers. Cars from most European countries (including Britain, Germany and Austria) are presumed to be fully insured, so no extra documentation is needed. To be safe, carry proof of insurance.

**Road conditions.** Poland is not a great place to drive your own vehicle. For one thing, it is reputed to have the highest accident mortality rates in Europe; in addition, roads are generally in poor condition (one publication estimates 45 percent of roads in Warsaw to be in disrepair) and often crowded. There is no system of motorways crisscrossing the country (there is just one 'superhighway', a toll road between Kraków and Katowice), so driving can be slow-going, since cars often have to compete with trucks and every other vehicle on the road.

Drivers should exercise care, particularly on roads in the countryside, which are often narrow, badly lit at night, and frequently under repair, especially in the summer months. You may find that country roads are used by pedestrians and animals as well as by vehicles. Heavy alcohol consumption can often be a contributing factor in accidents.

**Rules and regulations.** Drive on the right and pass on the left, but be careful at all times. Cars must be fitted with a nationality plate or sticker. A set of spare bulbs, a first-aid kit, and a warning triangle are also obligatory. Seat belts are compulsory in front and back seats; children under 12 are prohibited from travelling in the front seat and must be in car safety seat. Motorcycle riders and passengers must wear crash helmets. Using a mobile phone while driving is prohibited. Drinking and driving laws are tough; an amount of alcohol in the bloodstream above 0.02 percent is a punishable violation. Lights must be kept on at all times.

Speed limits are 130km/h (80mph) on motorways, 110km/h (69mph) on dual carriageways, 100km/h (60mph) on single carriageways, 90km/h (55mph) outside of urban areas, and 50km/h (30mph) in built-up areas (including Warsaw). You may be fined on the spot for speeding.

**Fuel costs** *(benzyna)*. Petrol (gas) stations are common along highways and main roads, but don't venture down minor roads without filling up. Stations are usually open 24 hours. Unleaded fuel is widely available (about 4.20 zł). Only in the rarest of cases are credit cards not accepted for payment.

**Parking.** Parking is a major problem in any of the big cities, especially where historic centres are pedestrian-only. If you are driving, check that your hotel has parking facilities. A car parked in a prohibited zone will be towed away. Only guarded car parks should be used.

**If you need help.** For roadside assistance, call Polish Road Assistance, tel: 071 9637, who can give you the number of the nearest roadside recovery service. Remember to put out the red warning triangle 50m (55yd) behind your car or 100m (110yd) behind if you are on a dual carriageway. If anyone is injured, the police must be notified. A safety infoline in various languages is available, tel: 0800 200 300 from a landline or payphone, or tel: +48 608 59 99 99 from a mobile phone.

**Road signs.** Standard international pictographs are in use all over Poland. A sign with 'Czarny Punkt', showing a cross in a black circle, indicates a very dangerous area.

| | |
|---|---|
| car | auto/samochód |
| unleaded fuel | benzyna bezołowiowa |
| parking | parking |
| detour | objazd |
| petrol/gas | benzyna |
| petrol station | stacja benzynowa |
| repair | naprawić |
| breakdown | awaria |
| no passing | zakaz wyprzedzania |

## E

## ELECTRICITY

The current is 220 volts AC, 50 Hertz throughout Poland. Plugs are the standard continental (two-prong) type, for which British and North American appliances need an adapter. Electrical equipment of 110V/60Hz requires an adapter or voltage converter.

## EMBASSIES AND CONSULATES

Embassies are located in Warsaw; a few nations have consulates in other cities, notably Kraków and Gdańsk.

**Australia:** Embassy, ul. Nowogrodzka 11, tel: 022 521 3444.
**Canada:** Embassy, ul. Matejki 1–5, 10th floor, tel: 022 584 3100.

**Ireland:** Consulate (Warsaw), ul. Mysia 5, tel: 022 849 6655.

**New Zealand:** Embassy, Al. Ujazdowskie 51, tel: 022 521 0500.

**South Africa:** Consulate (Warsaw), ul. Koszykowa 54, tel: 022 625 6228.

**UK:** Embassy, Al. Róż 1, tel: 022 311 0001. Consulate (Kraków), ul. Św. Anny 9, tel: 012 421 7030.

**USA:** Embassy, Al. Ujazdowskie 29–31, tel: 022 625 1401. Consulate (Kraków), ul. Stolarska 9, tel: 012 424 5100.

## EMERGENCIES

The three main emergency services telephone numbers are listed below, although the chances of an English speaker at the other end are slim.

**Ambulance** tel: 999
**Fire** tel: 998
**Police** tel: 997

| | |
|---|---|
| ambulance | **karetka pogotowia** |
| doctor | **lekarz** |
| hospital | **szpital** |
| police | **policja** |
| Can you help me? | **Czy może mi pan[i] pomóc?** |

## G

## GAY AND LESBIAN TRAVELLERS

As a fervently Catholic and conservative country, gay life is not much out in the open in Poland. Still, there are gay scenes in Warsaw and Kraków and to a lesser extent in smaller cities. A good organisation to contact in Warsaw is Lambda (ul. Hoża 50/40, tel: 022 628 5222, < http://warszawa.lambda.org.pl>). For information on gay Poland, check out <www.gay.pl> and <www.gejowo.com.pl>.

## GETTING THERE

**Air travel.** The major European airlines service Poland, as do the major American and Canadian carriers. The Polish national carrier, LOT Polish Airlines, flies from most major European cities and from North America. Scheduled flights are also available from British Airways. From the northeast coast of the US, flying time to Warsaw is about 8 hours.

**International airport.** Warsaw's Okęcie airport is the primary international airport, though those in Kraków, Gdańsk, Poznań, and others also handle a few international flights. Kraków's Balice International Airport has been refurbished and its capacity for international flights expanded.

**Rail travel.** Warsaw and Kraków, among other cities, can easily be reached from any major Western, Central or Eastern European city. From the UK, trains depart from London's Victoria station, arriving at Warsaw some 30 hours later. The most direct route is via Dover to Ostend and Berlin or Prague.

The following international rail passes are valid in Poland: InterRail, Euro Domino, EurailPass (and its variants), European East Pass and Polrailpass. In the US tel: (800) 4 EURAIL.

Warsaw's international railway station is Warszawa Centralna (tel: 9436). In Kraków, it is Kraków Główny (tel: 9436).

**By car/coach.** Warsaw is connected by major highway to Berlin, Prague, Budapest and Vienna. The cheapest way to get from London to Warsaw is by coach, which takes just short of a day and a half. Eurolines, <www.eurolines.com>, and other European bus companies make the trek, as do Polish companies such as Pekaes (tel: 022 626 9352) and Orbis Transport (tel: 022 827 7140). If you plan to drive across the Continent, the most direct route is via Ostend, Brussels and Berlin. Buses from across Europe arrive at Warszawa Zachodnia (Warsaw West) station (tel: 022 822 4811).

## GUIDES AND TOURS

A good number of travel agencies and organisations in many countries operate organised sightseeing tours of Poland. A few offer specialised trips, such as Jewish pilgrimage religious-oriented tours. Other speciality tours include Schindler's List tours in Kazimierz, the historic Jewish quarter of Kraków.

Poland's largest tour operator Orbis offers everything from city tours and day trips to best-of-Poland trips, as do most travel agencies. For foreign-language guides and guided tours in major cities, contact the tourism information office or local office of the travel agent PTTK.

# H

## HEALTH AND MEDICAL CARE

Polish doctors and other health officials are generally knowledgeable and skilled, and most speak some English and German. Doctors and hospitals may expect immediate cash payment for health services. although medical treatment will normally be provided free of charge to EU citizens who have a European Health Insurance Card (available from post offices in the UK and online at <www.ehic.org.uk>). Visitors from non-EU countries should obtain medical insurance, and even EU citizens may wish to insure themselves privately, for example to ensure prompt repatriation in a medical emergency.

As a matter of precaution, bottled water is recommended and is inexpensive to buy. If you plan to spend a lot of time in country areas, particularly those close to Russia, Lithuania or Belarus, it is wise to see your doctor about the symptoms and treatment of Lyme Disease.

Emergency medical treatment on the scene is available for foreigners. Ask at your hotel or consulate for the name of a doctor who speaks your language. In Warsaw, Kraków, Gdańsk, Katowice, Szczecin, Łódź and Poznań, call Falck using the local city code followed by 9675, which can usually arrange English-language emergency services. Warsaw's Central Emergency Medical Centre is located at ul. Hoża 56 (corner of ul. Poznańska). A private hospital with a good reputation is the Hospital of the Ministry of Internal Affairs (ul. Wołoska 137, tel: 022 508 1552). Centrum Medicover has medical centres in various Polish cities, such as Kraków, Warsaw, Poznań and Gdańsk; in emergencies tel: 9677 (24 hours).

**Pharmacies.** Look for the sign *apteka*. In Poland these shops only sell pharmaceutical and related products. Tourism Information Offices have lists of night pharmacies. In Warsaw, two are: Apteka (ul. Puławska 39, tel: 022 849 3757) and Apteka (al. Jerozolimskie 54, Centralny Station, tel: 022 825 6986). Local editions of *In Your Pocket*, <www.inyourpocket.com>, list additional pharmacies.

| | |
|---|---|
| Where's the nearest pharmacy? | **Gdzie jest najbliższa apteka?** |
| I need a doctor. | **Ja potrzebuję doktora.** |
| I need a dentist. | **Ja potrzebuję dentystę.** |

## HOLIDAYS

| | |
|---|---|
| 1 January | New Year's Day |
| March/April | Easter |
| 1 May | Labour Day |
| 3 May | Constitution Day |
| June | Corpus Christi |
| 15 August | Assumption |
| 1 November | All Saints' Day |

11 November     National Independence Day
24–25 December     Christmas

## I

## INTERNET CAFÉS

Internet cafés are very popular in Poland's bigger cities, and prices are very inexpensive, from 4–6 zł/hour.

**Warsaw:** Casablanca (ul. Krakowskie Przedmieście 4–6, tel: 022 828 1447); Cyber Café (ul. Żwirki i Wigury 1, inside the Courtyard Marriott hotel opposite the airport, tel: 022 650 0172); Silver Zone (ul. Puławska 17, tel: 022 852 8888).

**Kraków:** Garinet (ul. Floriańska 18, tel: 012 423 2233); PcNet (ul. Kościuszki 82, tel: 012 411 2688).

## L

## LANGUAGE

Polish, a Slavic language, is the mother tongue of 99 percent of the population. The most widely known foreign language is German, though English is quickly gaining on it and is far more popular than German among younger people. In the cities English speakers are unlikely to find many problems, as most people they'll encounter speak at least some English (many Poles are fluent in English and other languages). In the countryside, communication difficulties are to be expected. The Polish language is extremely difficult, but learning even a handful of key phrases is a good idea and will prove helpful. As a general rule, the accent falls on the second-last syllable.

The following are a few useful phrases and some signs you are likely to see:

| | |
|---|---|
| yes | tak |
| no | nie |
| Hi. (informal, singular/plural) | Cześć. |
| Good night. | Dobranoc. |
| Goodbye. | Do widzenia. |
| Thank you (very much). | Dziękuję (bardzo). |
| Excuse me (sorry). | Przepraszam. |
| Do you speak English? | Czy Pan/Pani mówi po angielsku? |
| I don't understand. | Nie rozumiem. |
| I understand. | Rozumiem. |
| I don't know. | Nie wiem. |
| Where is...? | Gdzie jest...? |
| How do I get to...? | Jak dojechać do...? |
| Good morning/day. | Dzień dobry. (jen doe-bri) |
| Good evening. | Dobry wieczór. (do-bri vee-a ye-chor) |
| Please. | Proszę. (pro-sha) |
| Help! | Pomocy! (po-mo-tsay) |
| Hi/bye. | Cześć. (chesh) |
| Where is the toilet? | Gdzie są toalety? |
| May I have...? | Czy mogę...? |
| entrance | wejście |
| exit | wyjście |
| open | otwarte |
| closed | zamknięte |
| pharmacy | apteka |
| post office | poczta |
| avenue | Aleja (Al.) |
| street | ulica (ul.) |
| city centre | centrum |
| old town | stare miasto |

## M

### MAPS

Tourism Information Offices *(see page 170)* routinely supply visitors with free maps of cities (and regions, often for a nominal fee) that are sufficient for most peoples' purposes. There are plenty of more comprehensive maps available, published by PPWK and others. Those driving through Poland may want to purchase a Road Atlas (Atlas Samochodowy).

### MEDIA

**Newspapers and magazines.** *The Warsaw Voice*, published weekly, is probably the most authoritative English-language newspaper. It gives a good insight into Polish politics, business and culture and also has a listings section for tourists. Other papers to look for include *Welcome to Warsaw* (a free information magazine), *Warsaw Insider* (free quarterly with cultural listings) and *In Your Pocket* (Warsaw, Kraków and Gdańsk editions – mini-guides with lots of listings and pertinent information). Western newspapers, including *The International Herald Tribune, Financial Times* and *USA Today*, arrive the day of publication. Others may arrive a day or two late.

**Radio and television.** Polish Radio 1, at varying frequencies across Poland, broadcasts headline news in English. There are two Polish state television channels and PolSat, a private channel. All hotels with four or more stars (and some three-star hotels) offer satellite television with major European and American channels and news programmes.

### MONEY

**Currency.** The unit of currency is the złoty (zł). Coins in circulation include 1, 2 and 5 zł. Banknotes come in denominations of 10,

## Numbers

| | | | |
|---|---|---|---|
| zero | **zero** | eleven | **jedenaście** |
| one | **jeden** | fifteen | **piętnaście** |
| two | **dwa** | sixteen | **szesnaście** |
| three | **trzy** | seventeen | **siedemnaście** |
| four | **cztery** | eighteen | **osiemnaście** |
| five | **pięć** | nineteen | **dziewiętnaście** |
| six | **sześć** | twenty | **dwadzieścia** |
| seven | **siedem** | thirty | **trzydzieści** |
| eight | **osiem** | forty | **czterdzieści** |
| nine | **dziewięć** | fifty | **pięćdziesiąt** |
| ten | **dziesięć** | hundred | **sto** |

20, 50, 100 and 200 zł. One złoty equals 100 groszy (gr), which you'll see in 1, 2, 5, 10, 20 and 50 coin denominations.

**Currency exchange.** Foreign currency can be exchanged (look for the signs marked *kantor*) at the airports and banks, as well as most hotels. *Kantors* only exchange cash and can be very informal-looking places. They offer the best rates (no commission). Your passport is only necessary when changing money at banks. It's wise to keep all your exchange receipts until you leave the country. The exchange rate at the time of writing is around 3.5 zł to the US dollar and 6 zł to the pound. There is no black market for currency in Poland; any offers from strangers to exchange money should be refused as this will be counterfeit. The Polish word for cash is *gotówka*.

**Credit cards.** Major international credit cards (Visa, Mastercard and American Express) are increasingly accepted in hotels, restaurants and shops, but are not accepted everywhere. In some cases, only one of the above credit cards will be accepted. You are usually unable to pay with a credit card at small supermarkets, museums and minor train stations.

**ATMs.** Cash machines *(bankomat)*, taking PLUS, Cirrus and most other major credit cards, are widespread in Polish cities and offer competitive international exchange rates. They dispense cash in Polish zł; a few also give cash in euros.

**Travellers cheques.** These may be cashed at all of the above outlets except *kantors* and may sometimes be substituted for cash, but you'll almost certainly get a much poorer rate of exchange than if you convert them to cash. Commission is generally 1 to 2 percent.

## OPENING TIMES

Opening times vary, but most businesses in Poland are open 8am–5pm Monday to Friday. Supermarkets, department stores and shopping centres are open 9am–8pm, Monday to Saturday; Sunday, 10am–6pm. Smaller shops are open 10am–6pm Monday to Friday, 9 or 10am–11 or 12pm Saturday. Some close all day Saturday, and almost all shut on Sunday. 'Non-Stop' signs mean 24-hour shopping.

Banks are generally open 9am–4pm Monday to Friday (some close at 1pm on Friday). Museums are usually closed on Monday, and are open 10am–5pm Tuesday to Sunday. Post offices are open 8am–8pm Monday to Friday, 8am–2pm Saturday. The Central Post Office in Warsaw is open 24 hours.

| | |
|---|---|
| Monday | **poniedziałek** |
| Tuesday | **wtorek** |
| Wednesday | **środa** |
| Thursday | **czwartek** |
| Friday | **piątek** |
| Saturday | **sobota** |
| Sunday | **niedziela** |

## P

**POLICE** *(policja)* (see also CRIME & SAFETY and EMERGENCIES)

Police emergency, tel: 997 or 112 from a mobile.
Warsaw Police Headquarters: ul. Wilcza 21.

| police station | **posterunek policji** |
|---|---|

## POST OFFICES

Post offices *(poczta)* handle mail, telephone, telegraph, telex and (at the larger offices) fax. Stamps can also be purchased at newsagents or in stores where postcards are sold. Red mailboxes on the street are marked 'Poczta'.

The Central Post Office (Urząd Pocztowy Warszawa 1) in Warsaw (ul. Świętokrzyska 31–3, tel: 022 505 3316) is open 24 hours a day. Other useful branches are at Targowa Street (ul. Targowa 73, tel: 022 590 0360), Konstytucji Square (pl. Konstytucji 3, tel: 022 621 4825) and Old Market Square (Rynek Starego Miasta 15, tel: 022 831 2333).

In Kraków, the main Post Office is located at (ul. Westerplatte 20, tel: 012 422 3991; open Mon–Fri 7.30am–8.30pm, Sat 8am–2pm, Sun 9am–2pm). A second branch is opposite the train station, at (ul. Lubicz 4; open Mon–Fri 24 hours, with some services restricted 8pm–7am, Sat 7am–8pm).

International postcards and letters to Europe cost 1.90 zł; to the US and Canada, 2.10 zł.

DHL, TNT and UPS all have offices in Warsaw and in Kraków.

| letter | **list** |
|---|---|
| stamp | **znaczek** |
| air mail | **poczta lotnicza** |

## PUBLIC TRANSPORT

### Local transport

Most Polish cities have well-developed systems of public transport that include buses and trams (and in the case of Warsaw, a single Metro, or subway, line).

In Warsaw, 1,200 buses operate from 5am to 11pm; night buses go from 11.30pm to 5.30am. Tickets (valid on buses, trams and the Metro) can be purchased at kiosks with a green-and-yellow Ruch logo, and you can also buy a ticket directly from the driver for a slightly higher price. Validate your ticket upon boarding (old punch-cards are being phased out in favour of magnetic-strip cards). Ticket inspectors have the power to issue fines on the spot for travelling without a validated ticket.

In Kraków, there are 22 tram lines and more than 100 bus lines. They run from 5am to 11pm. You can purchase single-trip tickets, one-hour tickets, one-day and one-week passes.

**Buses** (*autobus*). Most city buses are red. Fast buses and night buses are twice as expensive as normal day buses. Signal that you want to get off by pressing the bell.

**Trams** (*tramwaj*). Trams, or streetcars, cover large networks in most Polish cities; some run throughout the night. Departure schedules are posted, though they may not be strictly adhered to. In Warsaw, there's an Old Town tram that begins and ends its route at Castle Square, taking a 30-minute guided trip through the Old and New Towns.

**Taxis** (*taksówka*). Taxi fares should start at 5 zł and go up by about 1.4 zł every additional kilometre (at night, 2 zł). Polish taxis are notorious for overcharging foreigners. Unofficial taxis are ubiquitous, and very difficult for the uninitiated to tell apart from registered, legal cabs. The unofficial taxis line up at airports and train stations with impunity. If you want a taxi, you should always call for one; ask your hotel to call for you. For taxi company details, *see pages 147–8*. Hailing a cab is not recommended. Taxis hailed in the street will almost certainly be unofficial cabs. If it's an emergency, agree upon the fare in advance.

**Subway or underground** *(Metro)*. The Metro in Warsaw operates a single 13km (8-mile) line that runs from Plac Bankowy in the city centre to the southern suburb of Kabaty (near Ursynów). It functions daily 5am–11.15pm, with trains every 5 minutes during rush hour, every 8 minutes during off-peak hours.

**Transport around the country**
**Buses/coaches** *(autobus)*. The main bus station in Warsaw is Warszawa Zachodnia (Warsaw West, Al. Jerozolimskie 144, tel: 022 822 4811). Kraków's main bus station is by the train station (pl. Kolejowy, tel: 012 422 3134). Gdańsk's bus station is Dworzec PKS (ul. 3 Maja 12, tel: 058 302 0532) adjacent to the train station.

The national bus service, PKS, has the most extensive network of bus routes throughout the country. A private alternative is Polski Express (tel: 022 854 0285, <www.polskiexpress.pl>).

For bus information, tel: 0 300 300 300.

**Trains** *(pociąg)*. With over 26,500km (16,450 miles) of railway lines, the Polish railway network covers the whole country, making trains by far the most common and best way to travel between major cities. The exception is short journeys, when buses can be faster (Kraków to Zakopane, for example). Warsaw has six railway stations; most international trains arrive at Warszawa Centralna (Al. Jerozolimskie 54, tel: 022 9436), while others go to Warszawa Wschodnia. Smaller stations, mostly on the edges of the city, handle regional routes.

Kraków's main railway station is Kraków Dworzec Główny (Pl. Dworcowy 1, tel: 012 9436); it handles international and inter-city routes. Gdańsk's railway station is Gdańsk Główny (ul. Podwale Grodzkie 1, tel: 058 9436); a commuter train travels among the three components of the Tri-city, leaving every 10 minutes between 6am and 7.30pm and less frequently thereafter.

The rail journey from Warsaw to Kraków takes 3 hours; from Warsaw to Gdańsk, 3 hours 40 minutes; and from Warsaw to Poznań, 3 hours 20 minutes.

Tickets can be purchased at the train station in advance or on board from the conductor (for a surcharge).

For train timetables and information, visit <www.pkp.com.pl>.

| | |
|---|---|
| railway station | **dworzec kolejowy** |
| bus stop | **przystanek** |
| ticket kiosk (buses/trams) | **sprzedaż biletów MPK** |
| reserved seat ticket | **miejscówka** |
| departure | **odjazd** |
| arrival | **przyjazd** |
| Please, a ticket to… | **Proszę bilet do…** |
| return ticket | **bilet powrotny** |

## R

## RELIGION

Nearly all native Poles are Roman Catholic, and as many as 80 percent are practising Catholics. The late Pope John Paul II was a Cardinal and Archbishop of Kraków before becoming the head of the Catholic Church. Mass is said in Polish.

Other minority faiths, notably Protestant, Eastern Orthodox and Jewish, are represented in Poland. Tourism Information Offices should have a list of services held in English and other languages (infrequent).

## T

### TELEPHONES *(telefon)*

Most public telephones in Poland are now of the phone-card only type – although that doesn't mean that all of them are in working order. Phone cards, of which there are countless varieties, may be purchased at newsstands, some hotels, post offices and tourist information (IT) offices. Long distance and international calls can also be made in Warsaw at Netia Telephone (ul. Poleczki 13, tel: 022 330 2000) and TPSA (ul. Nowy Świat 6–12, tel: 022 627 4081). In Kraków, Netia Telephone (ul. J. Conrada 51, tel: 012 290 1143).

To make an international call from a public phone, dial the international access code (0 – listen for tone – 0-tone), followed by the country code and telephone number, including area code. There are no off-peak rates for international calls. For long-distance national calls, dial the area code (preceded by zero) and number; off-peak rates start at 10pm. Local calls do not require the area code. Mobile telephone numbers have 10 digits.

**International dialing code for Poland:** 48
**Local and regional directory assistance:** 913
**International directory assistance:** 908

**Area codes:**

| | |
|---|---|
| Gdańsk/Gdynia/Sopot | 058 |
| Kraków | 012 |
| Łodź | 042 |
| Poznań | 061 |
| Toruń | 056 |

| | |
|---|---|
| public telephone | **automat telefoniczny** |
| telephone card | **karta telefoniczna** |

| Warsaw | 022 |
|---|---|
| Zamość | 084 |
| Zakopane | 018 |

## TIME ZONES

All of Poland is in the same time zone, Central European Time, or Greenwich Mean Time + 1 hour (or US Eastern Standard Time + 6 hours). Daylight saving time in summer (GMT + 2) is in effect from the last Sunday in March.

| New York | London | **Warsaw** | Jo'burg | Sydney | Auckland |
|---|---|---|---|---|---|
| 6am | 11am | **noon** | noon | 8pm | 10pm |

## TIPPING

Tipping is the norm in Poland but not obligatory. It's customary to leave 10–15 percent at restaurants and round up the bill at bars. Some restaurants may add on a 10 percent tip; look carefully at the bill and ask if this appears to be the case to avoid tipping twice. Porters, maids and tourist guides also expect tips.

| bill/check | **rachunek** |
|---|---|

## TOILETS

In Poland public toilets *(toaleta publiczna)* can be few and far between. A small charge (1–2 zł) is common, and even cafés may still

| men's room | **męski (panowie)** |
|---|---|
| women's restroom | **damski (panie)** |
| free | **wolny** |
| occupied | **zajęty** |

charge patrons for use of their facilities. Men's rooms are commonly denoted by triangle symbols; women's rooms are denoted
by circles.

## TOURIST INFORMATION

Ranging from desks tucked away in the corners of obliging travel
agencies, to dedicated buildings complete with interactive maps and
more useful information than you could shake a stick at, Polish
tourist information centres should be your first port of call when
arriving at a destination. As well as being able to help you plan your
itinerary, most places also offer help and advice on accommodation,
car hire, the best places to eat authentic local food as well as a whole
host of other useful services. Below are details of tourist information offices in the key cities.

**Warsaw.** There are two tourist offices at Okęcie airport: in the
Terminal 1 arrival hall and the Etiuda terminal (open daily
May–Sept 8am–8pm, Oct–Apr 8am–6pm). Two further branches
are at Central Railway Station (al. Jerozolimskie 54; open daily
May–Sept 8am–8pm, Oct–Apr 8am–6pm) and ul. Krakowskie
Przedmieście 39 (open daily May–Sept 9am–8pm, Oct–Apr
9am–6pm). For general tourist information, tel: 022 9431 or see
<www.warsawtour.pl>.

**Kraków.** The Cloth Hall (Rynek Główny 1; open daily 9am–5pm,
tel: 012 433 7310), <www.krakow.pl>.

**Gdańsk.** Centrum Informacji Turystycznej (ul. Długa 45, tel: 058
301 9151 and ul. Hewelisusza 27, tel: 058 301 4355; open Mon–Fri
9am–6pm), <www.gdansk.pl>.

**Łódź.** Centrum Informacji Turystycznej (ul. Piotrkowska 87, tel:
042 638 5956), <www.uml.lodz.pl>.

**Poznań.** Centrum Informacji Miejskiej (ul. Ratajczaka 44, tel: 061 9431 or 061 851 9645) and Tourism Information Centre (Stary Rynek 59, tel: 061 852 6156), <www.cim.poznan.pl>.

Official web addresses for other destinations listed in this book:
**Auschwitz** <www.auschwitz.org.pl>
**Bydgoszcz** <www.it.bydgoszcz.pl>
**Gdynia** <www.gdynia.pl>
**Kashubia** <www.kaszuby.pl>
**Kazimierz Dolny** <www.kazimierzdolny.pl>
**Malbork** < www.malbork.pl>
**Sopot** <www.sopot.pl>
**Toruń** <www.torun.pl>
**Wieliczka** <www.kopalnia.pl>
**Zakopane** <www.zakopane.pl>
**Zamość** <www.zamosc.pl>

**UK:** Polish National Tourist Office, Level 3, Westec House, West Gate, London W5 1YY, tel: 08700 675012, fax: 08700 675011, <www.visitpoland.org>.

**US:** Polish National Tourist Office, 5 Marine View Plaza, Hoboken, NJ 07030, tel: 201 420 9910, fax: 201 584 9153, <www.poland tour.org>.

# W

## WEBSITES

Some useful websites to help you plan your trip to Poland:
**www.polandtour.org** (Polish National Tourism Office)
**www.polishworld.com** (general information, news, culture)
**www.poland.net** (general site)
**www.polhotels.com** (on-line reservation system; car hire)

**www.hotelspoland.com** (hotel clearing house)

**www.warsawvoice.com.pl** (site of English-language weekly)

**www.inyourpocket.com** (*In Your Pocket* listings site)

**www.warsawinsider.pl** (*Warsaw Insider* site)

**www.orbis.pl** (Poland's largest tour and hotel company)

**www.krakow.pl** (Kraków site)

**www.warsawtour.pl** (Warsaw tourist information)

**www.gdansk.pl** (municipal site)

**www.pkp.com.pl** (Polish state railway schedules)

**www.polishvodkas.com** (self-explanatory)

## WEIGHTS AND MEASURES

Poland uses the metric system.

## Y

## YOUTH HOSTELS

There is an extensive network of youth hostels *(schroniska młod-zieżowe)* – reportedly as many as 950 in all – throughout Poland. For additional information, contact the Polish Association of Youth Hostels (ul. Chocimska 28, Warsaw, tel: 022 849 8128, <www.ptsm.org.pl>). International Student Hostels Accommodation is available through the ALMATUR Travel Bureau (ul. Kopernika 23, Warsaw, tel: 022 826 2639, <www.almatur.pl>).

Hostels in Warsaw include the extremely clean Agrykola (ul. Myśliwiecka 9, tel: 022 622 9105, <www.agrykola-noclegi.pl>) and the legendary Nathan's Villa (ul. Piękna 24–6, tel: 022 622 2946, <www.nathansvilla.com>).

In Kraków try City Hostel (ul. Św. Krzyża 21, tel: 012 426 1815, <www.cityhostel.pl>), the Communist-themed Good Bye Lenin (ul. Joselewicza 23, tel: 012 421 2030, <www.goodbyelenin.pl>) and, again, Nathan's Villa (ul. Św. Agnieszki 1, tel: 012 422 3545, <www.nathansvilla.com>).

# Recommended Hotels

Hotels in Poland are graded from one star to five stars, though the rating may weigh the condition of the building equally against other factors like services and rooms. Poland's roster of quality visitor accommodations has improved but, especially at the mid- to lower-range, choices can be limited. International chains and joint ventures have moved in to compete with the well-established hotels operated by big Polish chains like Orbis and Gromada. It is always wise to book ahead, particularly for June, July, August and September.

The following guide denotes the rack rate price of a double room with bath/shower in high season (May through October, as well as Christmas) including breakfast and VAT. Hotel room rates are variously quoted in US dollars, euros and Polish złoty – though the bill will ultimately be rendered in złoty. All accept major credit cards, except where noted.

Most local tourism information offices will also have lists of private accommodation.

| | |
|---|---|
| $$$$$ | over $200 |
| $$$$ | $120–200 |
| $$$ | $70–120 |
| $$ | $30–70 |
| $ | below $30 |

## KRAKOW

**Hotel Copernicus $$$$$** *ul. Kanonicza 16, tel: 012 424 3400, <www.hotel.com.pl>*. On one of Kraków's most atmospheric streets, this is one of the city's newest and grandest hotels. It is located in a marvellously restored 16th-century building just minutes from Wawel Hill. Rooms are very elegant, furnished with well-chosen antiques.

**Hotel Eden $$$** *ul. Ciemna 15, tel: 012 430 6565, <www.hotel eden.pl>*. A small and friendly new hotel leading a revival of the historic Jewish quarter, Kazimierz. Simple and modern furnishings in a renovated 15th-century building, with a sauna. Good pub, Ye Old Goat, downstairs.

**Hotel Francuski $$$$** *ul. Pijarska 13, tel: 012 627 3777, <www. orbis.pl>*. This handsome Orbis hotel, built in 1912, is on the edge of the Old Town, facing the Planty near the old city wall. Rooms are luxurious and traditional in style.

**Grand Hotel $$$$** *ul. Sławkowska 5/7, tel: 012 421 8360, <www.grand.pl>*. A stylish 19th-century hotel with stained-glass-lined hallways and classic furnishings, the Grand is one of the most impressive places to stay in Kraków. Situated in the heart of the Old Town, it offers lavishly furnished rooms and some extremely chic suites with period features. There's also an elegant Belle Époque restaurant.

**Guest Rooms Wielopole $$$** *ul. Wielopole 3, tel: 012 422 1475, <www.wielopole.pl>*. Excellent value accommodation two minutes east of the Old Town; facilities are clean and modern. More of a hotel than a guesthouse. Prices include free high-speed internet connection in every room.

**Hotel Maltański $$$** *ul. Straszewskiego 14, tel: 012 431 0010, <www.donimirski.com>*. A new, modern and elegant small hotel in a renovated 19th-century building conveniently located on the southwestern edge of the Planty. Classy rooms, good service and breakfast. In a quiet location within walking distance of Wawel Hill and all major sights.

**NorPol Apartments $$$** *ul. Szczepańska 7, tel: 012 431 1424, <www.norpol-apartments.com>*. Two modern apartments, one just north of the Old Town (sleeping up to six people) and the other in Kazimierz (sleeping up to nine). An above-average, good value choice if you're looking for a more relaxed, self-catering option. The website has good photographs and also shows availability.

**Pod Różą $$$$** *ul. Floriańska 14, tel: 012 424 3300, <www.hotel. com.pl>*. One of Kraków's most popular hotels is this mid-size charmer on famous Floriańska street. The 14th-century building has recently been totally renovated in a traditional style. Chandeliers and arched ceilings await guests.

**Hotel Pollera $$$** *ul. Szpitalna 30, tel: 012 422 1044, <www. pollera.com.pl>*. Art lovers will like this traditional 150-year-old hotel the moment they enter the lobby. A stained-glass window by Kraków artist Stanislaw Wyspiański hangs over the staircase. Rooms are old-fashioned but nicely equipped for the price. Close to the Opera House and Market Square.

**Hotel Polski $$$** *ul. Pijarska 17, tel: 012 422 1144, <www. podorlem.com.pl>*. A pleasant, medium-sized, quiet hotel, located in the historic centre of town. Restaurant.

**Hotel Rezydent $$$** *ul. Grodzka 9, tel: 012 429 5410, <www. rthotels.com.pl>*. A great location if you want to be in the thick of things: on the street with the most foot traffic leading off the Market Square. Appropriately ancient on the outside, fresh and modern on the inside. Triples and a huge apartment for four available.

**Hotel Saski $$$** *ul. Sławkowska 3, tel: 012 421 4222, <www. hotelsaski.com.pl>*. An enviably located old-style hotel in a 16th century building, smack in the middle of the Old Town, on one of its nicest streets. Rooms are either very traditional and very frilly, or rather modern.

## ZAKOPANE

**Hotel Belvedere $$$$$** *ul. Droga do Białego 3, tel: 018 202 1200, <www.belvederehotel.pl>*. Modern hotel built in the traditional, local style, with a sports centre including a swimming pool, squash court and gym. Three restaurants and a café provide plenty of choice. Within walking distance of Zakopane's centre.

**Hotel Litwor $$$–$$$$** *ul. Krupówki 40, tel: 018 201 7189, <www.litwor.pl>*. On a small square off Zakopane's main shopping promenade, this large, handsome traditional hotel is one of the choicest places to stay in town. It has a delightful lobby bar, great restaurant, nicely furnished rooms, an indoor swimming pool and fitness centre with sauna.

**Villa Marilor $$$$** *ul. Kosciuszki 18, tel: 018 206 4411, <www. hotelmarilor.com>*. A traditional, elegant country-house hotel in a central location, with a tennis court and large garden. The restaurant serves Polish and European cuisine.

## ZAMOSC

**Arkadia $$** *Rynek Wielki 9, tel: 084 638 6539, <www.polishin.pl>*. An enviable location, right on one of Poland's finest Renaissance market squares, this tiny hotel is a worthy alternative to the more upmarket Orbis hotel around the corner.

**Hotel Orbis Zamojski $$$** *ul. Kołłątaja 2–6, tel: 084 639 2516, <www.orbis.pl>*. This hotel, occupying six nicely renovated 16th-century townhouses next to the Town Hall on the magnificent Market Square, is one of the Orbis chain's best efforts. Stylishly modern, but respectful of the original architecture, the buildings are connected by lovely interior courtyards.

## WARSAW

**Hotel Campanile $$** *ul. Towarowa 2, tel: 022 582 7200, <www. campanile.com.pl>*. Inside the same huge building as two other hotels, the city-centre Campanile is starting to get a little tatty, but for value, service and facilities this one really is very hard to beat.

**Hotel Harenda $$–$$$** *Krakowskie Przedmieście 4–6, tel: 022 826 0071, <www.hotelharenda.com.pl>*. Great location near the university on one of Warsaw's finest streets, a few minutes' walk from the Old Town. Rooms are modern and plainly furnished. There's a lively pub (of the same name) next door.

**Kyriad Prestige Hotel $$$** *ul. Towarowa 2, tel: 022 582 7500, <www.kyriadprestige.com.pl>*. Next door to the excellent value

Campanile, Kyriad Prestige has one extra star but remains more or less the same as its neighbour with a few business-type extras such as a gym and a swanky bar that stays open late.

**Hotel Maria $$** *al. Jana Pawła II 71, tel: 022 838 4062, <www.hotelmaria.pl>.* A delightful family-run hotel near the Powązki and Jewish cemeteries and within walking distance of the Old Town. Friendly service and nicely furnished modern rooms; an especially good option for those who don't like big corporate hotels. The restaurant offers a good variety of Polish and European dishes and a well-chosen wine list.

**Marriott Warsaw $$$$$** *al. Jerozolimskie 65–79, tel: 022 630 6306, <www.marriott.com>.* Luxurious modern high-rise in the city centre, with 10 restaurants, health club, swimming pool and penthouse cocktail bar.

**MDM Hotel $$$$** *pl. Konstytucji 1, tel: 022 621 6211, <www.hotelmdm.com.pl>.* Large hotel centrally located on Constitution Square. The building is typical of 1950s Polish architecture, and the standard décor is a bit dated, but rooms are large and it's a fair deal for the location.

**Polonia Palace Hotel $$$$$** *al. Jerozolimskie 45, tel: 022 318 2800, <www.poloniapalace.com>.* One of Warsaw's oldest hotels, immaculately restored with a Belle Époque restaurant and various facilities, in a city centre location.

**Le Royal Méridien Bristol $$$$$** *ul. Krakowskie Przedmieście 42–4, tel: 022 625 2525, <www.warsaw.lemeridien.com>.* The most luxurious traditional hotel in Warsaw, this beautiful 1901 Beaux Arts building is elegantly furnished throughout. Within walking distance of the Old Town. Fitness centre, pool, sauna. Great café, restaurant.

**Sheraton Warsaw $$$$$** *ul. Prusa 2, tel: 022 657 6800, <www.sheraton.com.pl>.* The hotel of choice for international business travellers, the very modern and elegant Sheraton is located halfway between Łazienki Park and the Old Town. Rooms are luxuriously appointed, and 'executive rooms' are completely outfitted with work facilities. Excellent gym, restaurants, services.

## GDANSK

**Minihotel Abak $** *ul. Beethovena 8, tel: 058 322 0440, <www.abak.gda.pl>.* A bit of a trek from the city centre up a long steep hill, this superb value guesthouse provides clean, albeit basic facilities with the addition of a communal kitchen and the option to have restaurant food delivered to your room. Possibly the best budget option in the city.

**Dom Aktora $$** *ul. Straganiarska 55–6, tel: 058 301 6193, <www.domaktora.pl>.* This low-key pension in the heart of Main Town has a reputation as a boarding house for actors and theatre people. Rooms are utterly simple, but very clean.

**Hotel Hanza $$$$** *ul. Tokarska 6, tel: 058 305 3427, <www.hotelhanza.pl>.* One of Gdańsk's most luxurious options in the Main Town. On the waterfront (some rooms have river views), this modern hotel is also just minutes from the Long Market. Attractive and luxurious rooms with a clean aesthetic rather than fussy décor. Hairdressing salon and fitness centre with spa. Very good restaurant and cocktail bar.

**Holiday Inn Gdańsk $$$** *ul. Podwale Grodzkie 9, tel: 058 300 6000, <www.gdansk.azurehotel.pl>.* This large American chain hotel is just across from the Gdańsk railway station, and thus close to the highlights of the Main Town, the Old Town and the now-quiet shipyards. Good service, quality business facilities, standard but well-equipped rooms.

**Mercure Hevelius Gdańsk $$$** *ul. Heweliusza 22, tel: 058 321 0000, <www.orbis.pl>.* Within walking distance of the Old Town, this comfortable modern hotel has a good restaurant, beauty salon, massage parlour, solarium and nightclub. Being a high-rise, the hotel provides great views from the guestrooms.

## SOPOT

**Pensjonat Wanda $$** *ul. Poniatowskiego 7, tel: 058 550 3038,* <*www.bws-hotele.pl*>. Perfectly located by the beach and near the pier, this pension occupies a period building, with sauna and solarium.

**Sofitel Grand Hotel $$$** *ul. Powstancóv Warszawy 12–14, tel: 058 520 6000,* <*www.orbis.pl*>. Most appropriately named, this impressive red-roofed hotel, a 1927 Art Nouveau landmark, sits facing the Gdańsk Bay in the chic seaside resort of Sopot. The hotel is refined but not pretentious. A surprisingly good deal.

## TORUN

**Hotel Petite Fleur $$** *ul. Piekary 25, tel: 056 663 4400,* <*www. petitefleur.pl*>. A new, cosy little hotel in the heart of Toruń's Old Town, just two blocks from the Market Square. The hotel occupies two elegant Renaissance burgher's houses and has retained numerous period features. Rooms are large and comfortable. Very good restaurant downstairs in the cellar.

**Hotel Pod Orłem $$** *ul. Mostowa 17, tel: 056 622 5025,* <*www. hotel.torun.pl*>. Large for the tiny Old Town, this functional hotel near St Mary's Church is a perfectly fine place to stay, though it doesn't aim much higher than that. Decent restaurant.

**Hotel Zajazd Staropolski $$** *ul. Żeglarska 10–14, tel: 056 622 6060,* <*www.gromada.pl*>. One of the best options in the Old Town, between the Copernicus Museum and St Mary's Church, on an interesting street that leads to the river. Comfortable and friendly. Well-equipped rooms spread across three handsome townhouses. Good restaurant.

## BYDGOSZCZ

**Hotel Brda $$** *ul. Dworcowa 94, tel: 052 585 01 00* <*www.hotel brda.com.pl*>. A towering, Communist-era beauty providing a choice of both renovated and Cold War-feel rooms, free wireless internet and friendly staff between the train station and the Old Town. Ideal for those looking for the authentic small town Polish experience.

## POZNAN

**Brovaria $$$** *Stary Rynek 73–4, tel: 061 858 6868, <www.brovaria. pl>*. With views over the Old Market Square, this hotel combines stylish modernity with historic architecture. Good bar and restaurant.

**HP Park Hotel $$$** *ul. abpa A. Baraniaka 77, tel: 061 874 1100, <www.hotelpark.pl>*. A well-equipped, modern hotel on the banks of Lake Malta, south of Poznań's city centre. Perfect for trade-show attendees. Excellent, friendly service.

**Hotel Royal $$$** *ul. Św. Marcina 71, tel: 061 858 2300, <www. hotel-royal.com.pl>*. Set back from the busy shopping street of Św. Marcina in a quiet courtyard, this exceedingly handsome hotel is within easy walking distance of the Old Town. The staff are friendly and the rooms are large.

**Hotel Vivaldi $$$** *ul. Winogrady 9, tel: 061 853 8100, <www. vivaldi.pl>*. The Vivaldi is a modern, high-standard hotel, close to the city centre. Facilities include restaurant, café and swimming pool.

## KAZIMIERZ DOLNY

**Dom Architekta $$** *Rynek 20, tel: 081 883 5544, <www.dom-architekta.pl>*. Owned by the Polish Union of Architects with a great location on the Market Square.

**Hotel Stara Łaźnia $$** *ul. Senatorska 21, tel: 081 882 1340, <www. laznia.kazimierzdolny.pl>*. A small and friendly hotel, centrally located with a pretty good restaurant. Much in demand in high season.

**Hotel Zajazd Piastowski $$** *ul. Słoneczna 3, tel: 081 889 0900, <www.zajazdpiastowski.pl>*. A large and pleasant chalet-style hotel, a few kilometres beyond the town centre. Swimming pool and bicycle rental, horseback riding.

## Recommended Restaurants

The dining scene in Poland's cities has improved dramatically in recent years, and diners now have a wider choice of cuisines and types of restaurants than ever. The emphasis remains on Polish cooking, and for most visitors, delving into the national diet in restaurants both fancy and informal will be at the top of their list.

Book ahead wherever possible at top-tier restaurants in Kraków and Warsaw. Many restaurants remain open throughout the afternoon, and most stay open late, until 11pm or midnight. All the restaurants below accept major credit cards except where noted. The following guidelines denote an average three-course meal for one, excluding wine and service:

| | |
|---|---|
| $$$$ | over zł ($20+) |
| $$$ | 40–80 zł ($10–20) |
| $$ | 15–40 zł ($5–10) |
| $ | below 15 zł ($4 or less) |

## KRAKOW

**Café Ariel $$$** *ul. Szeroka 18, tel: 012 421 7920.* Open daily for breakfast, lunch and dinner. In the heart of Kazimierz, the Jewish quarter, is this charming long-established Jewish (but non-kosher) restaurant. Upstairs, it's decorated with lodge-like animal trophies, with nightly (8pm) performances by a klezmer music trio. Great fun.

**Café Camelot $$** *ul. Św. Tomasza 17, tel: 012 421 0123.* Open daily for breakfast, lunch and dinner. Fashionable and funky café – a good place to sip tea, have a beer or enjoy a light meal, including breakfast. Excellent salads, soups, sandwiches and desserts.

**Chimera $–$$** *ul. Św. Anny 3, tel: 012 423 2178.* Salad bar is open 7.45am–10pm, offering inexpensive salads and snacks. Smart restaurant opens noon–late, serving traditionally Polish cuisine. The house speciality is roast lamb in almonds, and for vegetarians, cauliflower purée with spinach.

**Chłopskie Jadło $$$** *ul. Św. Jana 3, tel: 012 429 5157.* Open daily for lunch and dinner. The name means 'Peasant Kitchen', an apt description of this excellent chain of rustic Polish restaurants. Fun, colourful, farmhouse décor and classic, robust foods, including soups, *pierogi*, fish and meat dishes, with half-litre beers, and accompanied by folk music – as if in the Polish countryside. Breakfast and free cake on Sundays.

**Cyrano de Bergerac $$$$** *ul. Sławkowska 26, tel: 012 411 7288.* Open Mon–Sat for lunch and dinner. An elegant cellar restaurant serving French food at French prices to the city's elite plus passing celebrities. A veritable institution if, of course, you can afford it.

**Da Pietro $$$** *Rynek Główny 17, tel: 012 422 3279.* Open daily for lunch and dinner. Right on the Market Square, in a delightful cellar, this is a good place to get an Italian fix without breaking the bank. Large portions and a good list of pastas.

**Metropolitan $$$** *ul. Sławkowska 3, tel: 012 421 9803.* Open daily for breakfast, lunch and dinner. A sleek, cosmopolitan setting, with varnished wood, leather chairs and separate dining rooms. Chic house drinks and creative international cuisine, such as sole with lime and chilli.

**Momo $** *ul. Dietla 49, tel: 060 968 5775.* Open daily for lunch and dinner. Wholesome, vegetarian food in a small and very informal restaurant between the Old Town and Kazimierz. One of the few places in the country to serve brown rice.

**North Fish $$** *Rynek Główny 25, tel: 012 431 1987.* Open daily for lunch and dinner. Quality fish and chips including spicy battered varieties and ketchup in an ice-cream cone. Added extras not found in the UK include an alcohol licence and decent salad bar.

**Padre $$** *ul. Wiślna 11, tel: 012 422 0866.* Open daily for lunch and dinner. A real gem of a restaurant tucked away in an old church cellar; the menu features a beguiling mix of decent Indian and Italian food. Good music policy too.

**Pod Aniołami $$$** *ul. Grodzka 35, tel: 012 421 3999.* Open daily for lunch and dinner. A cool and elegant medieval-looking cellar with stone walls, wood tables and rugs on the walls. There's also a breezy interior courtyard for outdoor dining in summer. Specialises in local cuisine, including all kinds of grilled meat dishes.

**Sphinx $$** *Rynek Główny 26, tel: 012 423 1140.* Open daily for lunch and dinner. Large plates of kebab-style dishes served with heaps of Polish cabbage in one of the country's most popular restaurant chains. Worth further investigation.

**Restauracja Szara $$** *Rynek Główny 6, tel: 012 421 6669.* Open daily for lunch and dinner. Elegant brasserie-style setting in an historic market square building, with various European dishes to enjoy.

**Wierzynek $$$** *Rynek Główny 15, tel: 012 424 9600.* Open daily for lunch and dinner. Kraków's most famous restaurant. Traditional Polish cuisine served in medieval buildings dating from 1364.

## ZAKOPANE

**Bąkowo Zohylina $$–$$$** *ul. Piłsudskiego 6, tel: 018 201 2045.* Open daily for lunch and dinner. This excellent highlander restaurant would be 'big fun', as my Polish friend likes to say, even if the food weren't terrific (which it is). The rustic décor – a wooden lodge with fur pelts and stuffed critters – is the perfect backdrop for dishes like sour cabbage soup and heavy portions of meat. A regionally costumed band plays mountain music with great showmanship.

**Gubałówka $$** *ul. Gubałówka 2, tel: 018 206 3630.* Open daily for lunch and dinner. Quality górale food served inside a large wooden lodge, or outdoors on the terrace in good weather, at the top of Zakopane's funicular train ride. What the place lacks in sophistication it more than compensates for with its stunning views of the mountains.

**Rooster $$** *ul. Zaruskiego 2, tel: 018 201 4738.* Open daily for lunch and dinner. Central and decidedly different, Rooster features a battalion of home-made 1950s Americana on the walls and a menu of classic American dishes with a typical Polish twist (served with cabbage). Popular with beer-swilling males.

## ZAMOSC

**Ratuszowa $** *Rynek Wielki 13, tel: 084 627 1557.* Open daily for lunch and dinner. This pretty basic restaurant-café is located in the Town Hall on Zamość's impressive Rynek, or Market Square, and is perfect for a beer, snack or simple Polish meal (such as ever-popular Polish sausages or soups) at very inexpensive prices.

**Restauracja Padwa $$–$$$** *ul. Staszica 23 (Rynek), tel: 084 638 6256.* Open daily for lunch and dinner. A cellar restaurant off the Market Square, it's like a dimly lit dungeon, with massive columns and arches and a vaulted ceiling. Though it has a vaguely pre-glasnost feel to it, with its glitzy 'drink bar' at one end, you can't go wrong with Padwa's upstanding Polish fare, such as *pierogi* and soups.

## WARSAW

**Adler $$$** *ul. Mokotowska 69, tel: 022 628 7384.* Open daily for lunch and dinner. This cosy, popular German restaurant revels in Wiener Schnitzel, sausages and German beers. Large portions and an occasionally noisy clientele (must be all that beer).

**Blue Cactus $$–$$$** *ul. Zajączkowska 11, tel: 022 851 2323.* Open daily for lunch and dinner. When Warsaw's ex-pats, many of whom are Americans, get an itch for tasty Tex-Mex (fajitas, enchiladas), they head to this colourful and cheery place.

**Le Cedre $$$** *al. Solidarności 61, tel: 022 670 1166.* Open daily for lunch and dinner. Like something out of *Lawrence of Arabia*, this immensely popular Lebanese restaurant titillates the taste buds with a menu of spicy meat dishes served with lashings of hot flat bread and of course the obligatory bubble pipe for afters. Belly dancing entertainment is sometimes provided.

**Champions $$$** *al. Jerozolimskie 65–79, tel: 022 630 5119.* Open daily for lunch and dinner. Like Tortilla Factory *(see page 186)*, Champions is as much a bar as a restaurant. Bursting with sports memorabilia, including a full-size boxing ring in the middle of the place, the food is mostly American and includes good ribs and vast burgers.

**Restauracja Dom Polski $$** *ul. Francuska 11, tel: 022 616 2432.* Elegant Polish cuisine served in a traditional villa, with its own charming garden for al fresco dining.

**Dyspensa $$$** *ul. Mokotowska 39, tel: 022 629 9989.* Open daily for lunch and dinner. An absolutely terrific-looking place decked out to look like a welcoming country kitchen. Very popular and atmospheric at night, when locals and a good many ex-pats pack it to enjoy international dishes including duck *à l'orange*.

**Gessler $$$–$$$$** *Rynek Starego Miasta 21–21a, tel: 022 837 0344.* Open daily for lunch and dinner. Another of the great-looking Polish restaurants in the Old Town Market Square, this comprises several rooms in the cellars of a townhouse, decorated like a country inn. Serves traditional and hearty Polish fare, rarely straying from game and meat.

**Malinowa $$$$** *ul. Krakowskie Przedmieście 42–44, tel: 022 551 1000.* Open daily for lunch and dinner. What you might expect from the opulent Bristol Hotel: a refined, traditional restaurant serving excellent Polish and French gourmet cuisine. One of the city's most luxurious and sophisticated dining rooms.

**Restauracja Polska Tradycja $$** *ul. Belwederska 18a, tel: 022 840 0901.* Beautifully decorated in an antique style, this townhouse restaurant has a wonderful selection of Polish dishes.

**Suparom Thai $$$** *ul. Marszałkowska 45–9, tel: 022 627 1888.* Open daily for lunch and dinner. This is certainly the best Thai restaurant in Warsaw. Great pad Thai and many other noodle-based dishes and soups in a friendly and attractive atmosphere.

**Tortilla Factory $$** *ul. Wilcza 46, tel: 022 621 8622.* Open daily for lunch and dinner. Tortillas and other classic Tex-Mex treats in an almost gastropub setting close to the city centre. Popular with a wide range of regular locals and expats, the food here is usually eaten as an afterthought once the beers start to flow – but that does-n't stop it from being one of the best places to eat in the capital.

## GDANSK

**Bar Pod Rybą $** *Długi Targ 35–8, tel: 058 305 1307.* Open daily for lunch and dinner. Tucked away up a side street off the street of its actual address, this magnificent little restaurant serves nothing but jacket potatoes to eat either in or as takeaway. Superb value and a visual treat, portions are both delicious and enormous. It gets busy during the week, but the wait is more than worth the ef-fort. Highly recommended.

**Green Way $$** *ul. Długa 11, tel: 058 301 8228.* Open daily for lunch and dinner. The central Gdańsk branch of Poland's most pop-ular vegetarian restaurant chain provides large dishes of interesting and experimental food at affordable prices to a diverse clientele of students, artists and pensioners. The best vegetarian option in town.

**Restauracja Kubicki $$–$$$** *ul. Wartka 5, tel: 058 301 0050.* Open daily for lunch and dinner. A homely, old-style establishment on the waterfront that is Gdańsk's longest-running family restaurant – since 1918. It serves the house speciality, 'Old Style Polish Knuckle', and meat, fish and poultry dishes in a place your grandparents might take you: deep red and gold wall coverings, dark wood and landscape paint-ings in gold frames – old-world charm.

**Kuchnia Rosyjska $** *ul. Długi Targ 11, tel: 058 301 2735.* Open daily for lunch and dinner. A cute little café on Gdańsk's most fa-mous street. Ideal for tasty meals of Russian food served in a themed setting.

**Restauracja Pod Łososiem $$$$** *ul. Szeroka 52–4, tel: 058 301 7652.* Open daily for lunch and dinner. Acclaimed as Gdańsk's finest formal restaurant, 'Under the Salmon' is a beautifully ornate establishment that used to be the distillery of Goldwasser vodka, which is infused with flecks of 23-carat gold. Posh and plush, with a sophisticated international menu, this is *the* place in Gdańsk for a special night out.

**Retman $$$–$$$$** *ul. Stagiewna 1, tel: 058 319 9248.* Open daily noon–midnight. Occupying a historic burgher's house near the waterfront and Royal Way, this appealing upmarket restaurant serves regional Polish specialities including borscht with lamb dumplings, trout and pike perch.

## SOPOT

**Wieloryb $$$** *ul. Podjazd 2, tel: 058 551 5722.* Open daily for lunch and dinner. Translating as The Whale, Wieloryb is a surreal dream of decoration and one of the most unusual-looking restaurants in Eastern Europe. Dishes run the gamut from seafood to ribs, but it's really the look of the place that marks this one out. Note that the doors are locked at 6pm. Ring the bell if you want to eat here during the evening.

## TORUŃ

**Hungaria $** *ul. Prosta 19, tel: 056 622 4189.* Open 10am–10pm. Polish and Hungarian cuisine. Located in the Old Town. Specialties include goulash soup and Hungarian-style poultry delicacies.

**Petite Fleur $$$** *ul. Piekary 25, tel: 056 663 4400.* Open daily for lunch and dinner. Serving sophisticated French and Polish cuisine, Toruń's most elegant restaurant is in the brick-walled cellar of a great boutique hotel in the Old Town. With heavy ceiling beams, romantic lighting and excellent service, it's the perfect place to celebrate a special occasion.

**Zajazd Staropolski $$** *ul. Żeglarska 10–14, tel: 056 622 6060.* Open daily for lunch and dinner. This laid-back and enjoyable family-style hotel restaurant serves reasonably good Polish fare under the attractive vaulted wooden ceilings of a 14th-century Gothic townhouse.

**Zielony Wieloryb $** *ul. Rynek Nowomiejski 13, tel: 056 653 9253*. Open daily for lunch and dinner. A maritime-style basement with a good selection of local and national favourites.

## BYDGOSZCZ

**Stary Port 13 $$** *ul. Stary Port 13, tel: 052 321 6208*. Open daily for lunch and dinner. Inside a wonderfully restored red-brick granary over-looking the Brda river, Stary Port 13 is arguably the best restaurant in town. The food is predominantly Polish, the décor includes a small working water wheel and there's often excellent traditional live music.

## POZNAN

**Bażanciarnia $$$** *Stary Rynek 94, tel: 061 855 3358*. Open daily for lunch and dinner. Beautifully decorated in an antique style, with an amazing collection of Polish classics on the menu. A superb choice.

**Gospoda Młyńskie Koło $$$** *ul. Browarna 37, tel: 061 878 9935*. Open daily for lunch and dinner. In a handsome old water mill in woods on the outskirts of town (5 minutes from the Market Square), this folksy restaurant serves Polish grilled specialities including boar and duck stuffed with apples. Great desserts and a lovely fireplace.

**Gospoda Pod Koziołkami $$$** *Stary Rynek 95, tel: 061 851 7868*. Open daily for lunch and dinner. Right on the Old Market Square, this comfortable and convenient restaurant has a simple self-service area upstairs, perfect for lunch, and an elegant dining room in the brick cellar. Polish standards.

**Ratuszowa $$$** *Stary Rynek 55, tel: 061 858 0513*. Open daily for lunch and dinner. Wonderfully atmospheric cellar restaurant on the Old Market Square. Decorated with theatre costumes and illuminated by candlelight. Elegant but hearty and rustic-flavoured Polish cooking with cheery service.

# INDEX

**Berlitz** pocket guide

# Poland

**Third Edition 2008**

Written by Neil Schlecht
Updated by Sco
Series Editor: Tony Halliday

**Photography credits**
Gregory Wrona: 6, 9, 10, 12, 15, 23, 28, 30, 33,
34, 35, 37, 41, 42, 44, 46, 48, 50, 51, 55, 61, 62,
64, 65, 66/7, 68, 69, 70, 71, 75, 76, 82, 86, 90, 92,
95, 101, 102, 104, 111, 112, 113, 115, 125, 126,
129, 134, 136, 137, 138, 143; Jerry Dennis: 17,
18, 24, 26, 39, 45, 56, 59, 78, 80, 83, 85, 87, 93,
94, 98, 106, 108, 109, 116, 118, 122, 132, 142;
Neil Schlecht 52, 72, 77, 96, 121, 127, 131, 139,
141; Kaplan Productions 21; János Kalmár 89

**Cover picture:** Michael Jenner/Robert
Harding

Printed in Singapore by Insight Print
Services (Pte) Ltd, 38 Joo Koon Road,
Singapore 628990. Tel: (65) 6865-1600.
Fax: (65) 6861-6438

Berlitz Trademark Reg. U.S. Patent Office
and other countries. Marca Registrada

**Contact us**

At Berlitz we strive to keep our guides as
accurate and up to date as possible, but if you
find anything that has changed, or if you have
any suggestions on ways to improve this guide,
then we would be delighted to hear from you.

Berlitz Publishing, PO Box 7910,
London SE1 1WE, England.
fax: (44) 20 7403 0290
email: berlitz@apaguide.co.uk
www.berlitzpublishing.com